The For

Anointing

Preparing for the Restoration of All Things

by

Eddie L. Lawrence, D. Min.

Title: **The Forerunner Anointing**
Sub-Title: **Preparing for the Restoration of All Things**

ISBN 1-59196-886-0

First Breath Ministries
P.O. Box 1228
Killen, Alabama 35645

Published by InstantPublisher.com

Cover Design by His Image Design
www.hisimage.com

First Printing, February, 2005

I wish I had had this book 20 years ago! Forerunners, you need not make the mistakes I made or live through the frustration I endured. You can now understand yourself, and others can begin to understand you. Though this book is very scholarly, it is amazingly practical and easy to read. *The Forerunner Anointing* will no doubt bring peace and strength to many who will finally understand this gift.

Dutch Sheets
Senior Pastor of Springs Harvest Fellowship in Colorado Springs, Colorado and Author of *Intercessory Prayer*

"Down through the ages God has been calling and anointing forerunners to birth new revelation from Heaven. Eddie Lawrence shines insightful light on these heroes of the faith and uses their stories to bring assurance to this present generation that God is indeed still calling and anointing forerunners to further His kingdom."

Lenny LeBlanc
Worship Leader and Dove Award Winning
Recording Artist

"Dr. Eddie Lawrence's book about the forerunner anointing is enthralling in the fullest sense of the word. This teaching by my pastor and mentor is bringing fresh revelation, impartation, and activation in my forerunner ministry to the nations. As I travel the world, I praise God I can see a new generation of people with the forerunner anointing preparing to reach the end time harvest. This is a great book giving practical assistance, support, and training to equip thousands of leaders to finish the unfinished task."

Leif Hetland
President of Global Missions Awareness and
International Conference Speaker

The Forerunner Anointing is a life changing message that brings clarity to our individual purpose and our corporate responsibility.

Karen Wheaton
Musical Recording Artist, Karen Wheaton Ministries

Contents

Foreword
By
Dutch Sheets

I functioned in the personality and mindset of a Forerunner before I knew I was one. In fact, I didn't know such a calling still existed. This meant that I didn't fully understand myself which, of course, created many problems and misunderstandings. I was frustrated much of the time and, as I look back honestly, am sure I was just as frustrating to people around me. I often wondered why I thought so differently than most of my friends and associates. For example, I:

- Saw perspectives that many never considered
- Asked questions that no one else seemed to care about
- Was more passionate or emotional than most
- Cared deeply about social issues, especially injustice
- Couldn't stand it when disorder existed
- Was extremely stubborn in my point of view

These and other ways of thinking made me an enigma to myself and to others. And, as with any gift or God-given motivation the inherent weaknesses, if not understood, can overshadow the strengths. This was certainly the case for me. When I found others not caring about an issue with the same intensity as I, my tendency was to become judgmental. I was very dogmatic, no gray areas existed anywhere. And, if it was wrong for me, it was wrong for everyone! If it was my passion or concern, it should have been everyone's!

Later, as I began to understand the ministry and mindset of a forerunner, the fog began to lift and many lights came on for me. I realized one could see an idea, point the way to it, and yet not be critical of those who didn't yet see or walk in the fullness of it. I realized, in fact, that God was often allowing me to see things before He began the process of revealing them to others. This didn't make me privileged, and certainly not more spiritual. It was simply that God intended for me to be a part of the revealing process – one of the forerunners through whom new directions and mindsets would be revealed.

Understanding these things enabled me to change my expectations toward others – without lowering the standard or ideal. I could declare a goal, prophetically stating where the Body of Christ needed to move toward, without judging them for not already being there or for not arriving fast enough. In short, understanding the calling, function and personality of a forerunner enabled me to *serve* the body of Christ, not *judge* them.

Oh, I still get frustrated and have to work at being content – a forerunner is never truly satisfied with progress. When others rejoice over ground gained they, rather than savor the process, are already seeing the next frontier that needs to be conquered. Forerunners never really arrive – they're always running ahead. But I'm gaining ground on my frustrations because I now understand my calling and temperament. I wish I had had this book 20 years ago!

Forerunners, you need not make the mistakes I made or live through the frustration I endured. You can now understand yourself, and others can begin to understand you. Though this book is very scholarly, it is amazingly practical and easy to read. *The Forerunner Anointing* will no doubt bring peace and strength to many who will finally understand this gift. The Body of Christ desperately needs the forerunners. Thank you, Dr. Lawrence, for your masterful job in helping us understand it.

Dutch Sheets
Senior Pastor of Springs Harvest Fellowship in Colorado Springs, Colorado, and author of the best selling book Intercessory Prayer.

Acknowledgments

I am so grateful to so many people who have spoken into my life and who have been used by the Lord to help me see what I need to see and hear what I need to hear. These have been forerunners bringing God's truth into my life. I could not possibly list them all here. Several people have been instrumental in this book coming into print.

My greatest appreciation, admiration, and the dedication of this book are reserved for my precious wife, Mikki. She, more than anyone else, has been my greatest earthly source of encouragement. I know of no one who lives for Christ as she does. I believe when her prayers arrive in Heaven they are immediately marked "priority." Thank you, Mikki, for the endless hours you have allowed me to be tucked away in my study, while you watched the children, handled calls, and prayed for me. Thank you for the way you encourage me to go deeper into the Word by sharing the insights you glean from the Scripture. What a joy to live with such a godly wife and mother!

I also want to thank my four children, Andrew, Kara Beth, Elliott, and Nathan for encouraging your Dad through the way you live your lives. You all are forerunners in the making, and I am very proud of you. You are such a joy to my life. Run farther than I have ever run!

A special thank you goes to Cathleen Wakeland, who at the time of this writing is forerunning as a missionary in Mozambique with Rolland and Heidi Baker and Iris Ministries. She gave sacrificially of her time and expertise in helping bring this work into form. Keep running, Cathleen!

I would like to express my appreciation for the wonderful congregation of Faith Tabernacle Church who encourage me Sunday by Sunday through their hunger and love for the Word of God. They heard this material first and received it gladly. I want to also thank our Granddaddy Pastor, Henry Melton, for being such a godly example for me to follow. Our personal intercessor, Tammy Alsup has also been such an encouragement to me through her exhortation, phone calls, footwork, and prayers for the completion of this work. Thanks, Tammy, for forerunning for me. Dan Blessing, my friend, and our executive administrator, has also supplied much encouragement to me along the way as well as taking care of hundreds of details at church while I studied, prayed, and prepared. Thanks for being a true armor bearer, Dan. Our church staff is the greatest and always encourages me in my teaching and preaching. You are all such a blessing. Thanks to Lenny LeBlanc, our worship leader, for speaking into my life and being such an encouraging brother.

To my friend and brother and our Missions Pastor, Leif Hetland who is a true pioneering forerunner, I appreciate you dear brother and thank you for the many times you have excitedly encouraged me concerning my teaching. Thank you for staying after me to get into print what you were hearing from the pulpit. Our Elders and Deacons have also encouraged me to keep forerunning for the whole congregation. Thank you!

Also, a special word of appreciation to Dutch Sheets who is a father, friend, and brother to me, as well as a true forerunner for our nation. Dutch, you have blessed me, and thank you for spiritually fathering so many of us to forerun for the King.

I must conclude these acknowledgements by expressing a written "thank you" to my Savior Jesus Christ, the ultimate forerunner, who is my friend, my elder brother and the Lord of my life.

Eddie Lawrence

Introduction

Life is filled with forerunners. At the moment you were conceived, you were a forerunner. When the conception in which you were created was about to take place, tens of millions of single cell spermatozoon were racing to implant themselves into the single egg inside your mother's womb, but you made it. You got there first. You outran the pack to become you. You are more than one in a million. You are carrying God-given destiny and the race toward that ultimate destiny continues. In one sense, we all started out forerunning.

Every field of endeavor has its forerunners. Someone got there first. Someone blazed a trail for others to follow. There are secular and spiritual forerunners. Let me throw some names at you and see if you do not associate them with events that opened up the way for others:

Neil Armstrong, Rosa Parks, Jonas Salk, Bill Gates, Sir Edmund Hillary, Orville & Wilbur Wright, Martin Luther King, Jr., Amelia Earhart, Charles Lindberg, Harriet Tubman, George Washington. Christopher Columbus, Ben Franklin, Lewis & Clark, Albert Einstein, Henry Ford, Dred Scott, Mahatma Gandhi, Christiaan Barnard, Galileo Galilei, John Glenn, George Washington Carver, and thousands of others.

Let's think back in the area of the Church and see if these names bring forth images of people who brought about a shift and took people into new territory. You may or may not agree with the direction they took, but you cannot deny the impact they made on others. Read through the list:

Martin Luther, Jonathan Edwards, Evan Roberts, Polycarp, Jean Guyon, John Knox, John Bunyan, Aimee Semple McPherson, Joseph Campbell, John Calvin, Joseph Arminius, John G. Lake, Charles Finney, John and Charles Wesley, William Seymour, Maria Woodworth-Etter, Billy Graham, Kathryn Khulman, Paul Yonggi Cho, Duncan Campbell, Nicholas Ludwig von Zindendorf, and thousands of others.

Each of the names on both lists represents a life that stepped beyond what was known as "normal" and did something, made something, went somewhere, said something, lived something, formulated something or restored something that so resonated in the hearts of other people that they are still known, respected, honored, or dishonored for what they did. Simply put, they influenced their culture with what they dared to do. They were forerunners. They prepared the way for others. The Bible is a book that contains the stories of some of God's greatest forerunners and of course the ultimate forerunner himself, Jesus. The forerunner spirit gets on people, and they begin to have a deep stirring inside of them to follow in the footsteps of Jesus.

Some people are just waiting to bolt out of the gates and race ahead of everyone else. They want others to go with them. Their minds have dreamed repeatedly about that place they know they are going to find once they bolt. They have visions of how it is going to be. It is not a rebellious motive that drives their heart, but it is a deep hungering craving that has gotten such a grip on them that they know they are ruined for anything else. They struggle with when to bolt, how to prepare to bolt, and even the "where to bolt?" question is fuzzy to them.

Nonetheless, that urge, that intense longing, that eagerness to begin the adventure into their God-given destiny is unrelenting. They know that the time to do it is getting closer. Their nostrils smell the quest in the wind that is beginning to whirl around in their spirits. They intuitively feel their spiritual muscles flexing, getting ready for the run. They have played the possible scenarios out in their minds over and over, contemplating how they will navigate the terrain of the adventure that God has mapped out for them. They feel it in their hearts. They always think they are ready before they really are. It's not that timing is not important, but to them, premature readiness is just desire that can't be contained.

Who are these strange breed of people who are so willing and ready to risk all for something they do not yet clearly see? Are they mere daredevils bored with life? Could it be that they are a chosen generation being stirred by the Spirit of God to seize this moment of history for a purpose far greater than their own lives could hold? Could it be that through their willingness to both live and die for their King that they clear and establish a landing zone in millions of human hearts for the return of the Lord of Lords and King of Kings Himself? Could this be a movement of the Spirit of God upon the hearts of a new army emerging to initiate the consummation of the restoration of all things? Many of these restless and yearning warriors are forerunners. They are called by God. They are right now in preparation. When they begin to bolt, watch out because an earth shaking and history shaping will be made more quickly than time can record. The birthing of the eternal purposes of God is about to unfold upon this generation of forerunners.

Let's look at some definitions of the word "forerunner." We will begin with some help from the American Heritage Dictionary. Some of the basic meanings of the term *forerunner* are:

a. One that precedes, as in time; a predecessor.
b. An ancestor; a forebear.
c. One that comes before and indicates the approach of another; a harbinger.
d. A warning sign or symptom.

In the context of sports, it is used to speak of "One who skis the course before the beginning of a race." Even the automobile industry has picked up this theme. Toyota 4Runners are seen on and off the highway. Obviously, this is a play on the word forerunner because a four-wheel drive vehicle is able to go in territory that the regular two wheelers cannot traverse. It can reach destinations that others cannot reach.

The word translated *forerunner* in the KJV and NKJV of the English Bible occurs just one time in Hebrews 6:20. It is given as a description of the work of the Lord Jesus Christ who went before us in death that he might bring us to the place of life. Jesus wins the forerunner contest hands down. He is absolutely the greatest forerunner of all times. Think of what he left, the distance he came, and what he did that no one else has ever done. He accomplished what no one else could have ever accomplished and paved the way for others to follow. He went beyond the veil of death into the presence of God, and intercedes for us as our Great High Priest. He dared to go where no man had gone before and returned as the conqueror of death, Hell, and the grave. Now that's what I call forerunning new territory. Let's look at how the writer of Hebrews describes this fascinating forerunning work of Jesus.

> *Hebrews 6:19 This hope we have as an anchor of the soul, both sure and steadfast, and which enters the Presence behind the veil, 20 where the forerunner has entered for us, even Jesus, having become High Priest forever according to the order of Melchizedek.*

The Greek word employed by the writer of Hebrews is the word **pródromos** (Strongs number 4274). *The Complete Word Study Dictionary* gives this definition for the word:

> To run ahead or before. The one running before. A forerunner, precursor, spoken of Jesus as entering before His followers into the celestial sanctuary (Heb 6:20). John the Baptist could be also taken as *ho pródromos* , the forerunner of the Lord Jesus, although he is not called that.

Jesus is the ultimate forerunner. Because he went where we could never have gone, we are now enabled to follow him there. He was also the first one to be resurrected from death never to die again. He is the first fruit and many will rise after him as they look unto him as the author and finisher of their faith.

The meaning of the word also helps us realize that there were many other forerunners in the Scripture. Noah was a forerunner who built the Ark that paved the way for humankind to continue to inhabit the earth. Abraham went out not knowing where he was going, yet it was based on a promise that millions of others would be blessed by his adventure of faith. Joseph, in a troubling set of circumstances, went ahead of his people to forerun and bring them to safety. Like Joseph, there are times when we go through seasons of pain and isolation, only to discover later that we were forerunning. Moses, Joshua, Rahab and others became forerunners because they did something that prepared the way for those who would follow them. All the Apostles of the New Testament were forerunners—sent ones who went ahead to establish something new and different. They were willing to suffer to establish what God had put in their hearts. They prepared the way for others. The longer I live the more I realize that the hand of God is orchestrating and weaving together the events, circumstances, and direction of our lives toward the fulfillment of His purposes. I love the message of Acts 17:26.

And He has made from one blood every nation of men to dwell on all the face of the earth, and has determined their preappointed times and the boundaries of their dwellings, ...

Let me personalize this for you. He determined when you would live and where you would live. He planted you here in this season on planet earth. He has ordained a purpose for your life, and He is going to work everything together for good as you love him and understand that you are called according to His purposes. He is going to conform you into the image of His own dear Son, and ultimately you will be with Him for all eternity. Inside this little bubble of time you call "now," it is important that you submit to the desires of His heart and lay your life at His feet for His purposes. In short, you need to allow Him to prepare you for He has prepared for you.

This book will present to you the premise that in these last days the Lord is releasing an anointing to raise up forerunners to herald the return of the Lord Jesus. The bulk of this work focuses on the characteristics of the forerunner anointing. Inside of you may very well be beating the heart of a forerunner. Read on and find out!

Chapter One
Preparing the Preparers

We are living in a season on planet Earth during which God is releasing a forerunner anointing to enable us to enter a time of radical shiftings, adjustments, and alignments that will be required of the body of Christ. God often reveals what He is about to do. God is beginning to disclose and reveal to people what He is about to do, and they in turn will be anointed to declare to the people of God what He is about to do on the Earth.

The term "forerunner," has been in use for years in conversations throughout the Christian community. But what is a forerunner *anointing*? What is God's purpose in bestowing it upon a person? The Bible is filled with information to help us understand the operation of this anointing.

The term "forerunner anointing" itself is not found in Scripture, but the lives of people who were forerunners can be found in Scripture. The expression forerunner anointing as used in this book refers to the Divine call, equipping, and enablement that rests on certain individuals to trek new territory, cut new paths, and clear out the thickets. These individuals will be used of the Lord to bring others into what God is doing now. They will be the first ones in on the "now" work of God.

Confused about what's Happening?

I once heard a story about a six-year-old first grader. Tommy started coming to school and telling his teacher and his classmates that he was going to have a little brother or a little sister. He was not sure yet which it was going to be, but he was going to have a little brother or a little sister. He was so exuberant and excited that he would tell them, every day or so, "I'm gonna have a little brother. I'm gonna have a little sister, and I'm so excited."

The time finally came when his mother called him into the room one day and said, "I want you to take your little hand and put it right here on Mommy's tummy." Tommy put his hand there, and he felt something move. He was startled and surprised. His Mom said, "Don't be surprised. This is your little brother or your little sister." Tommy didn't have much to say.

For several days at school Tommy was very quiet. His teacher noticed that he had not said anything in class for a week or so, and that he did not act as excited as he had been acting before. Finally one day she called him up near to her and said, "Now, tell me what's happened to this little brother or little sister of yours?" He started crying – big tears burst out of his eyes, and he said, "Teacher, I think Mommy ate it!"

When you do not know what's really happening in your life, you might react and respond in the wrong way, just as Tommy did. Instead of feeling joyful and excited, you might feel confused and upset. Father God understands this about you, and He often allows you to have previews of what He is about to do in your life so you won't feel so confused and upset.

Prophetic Previews

Surely the Lord God does nothing unless He reveals His secret counsel to His servants the prophets. Amos 3:7

In the Old Testament, Scripture tells us that God does nothing except He reveals it to his prophets. Who are his prophets? His prophets are those people whom God has ordained to declare His word and to speak forth what God is showing them or speaking to their heart. Amos 3:7 tells us that God – before He begins to move or do something – begins disclosing and revealing what He is about to do. The person He reveals it to is very often prophetic and is operating under what is called a forerunner anointing. The prophet Elijah operated under the forerunner anointing.

A voice is calling, "Clear the way for the Lord in the wilderness; Make smooth in the desert a highway for our God. Let every valley be lifted up, And every mountain and hill be made low; And let the rough ground become a plain, And the rugged terrain a broad valley;" Isaiah 40:3-4

15

Throughout the chronology of the whole Bible are examples of people whom God raised up and anointed so that they could release into the lives of others what God spoke to them.

Get Ready!

In the Old Testament, Isaiah prophesied that a voice would come crying out of the wilderness saying, "Prepare the way of the Lord." The content of this declaration is interesting. It was a declaration announcing, "Get ready – He is coming." It is saying, "Make a highway." God was calling through the Spirit to His people concerning the first coming of Jesus. He was saying, "I am putting together a construction crew. I want a good road when I get there. I do not want any mountains to have to overcome or any valleys to go through. I want a straight path." It was a call to the people of God – the King is coming. The Lord is on the way. His glory is going to be manifest. Get things in order. Get the rough places made smooth, get any obstacles out of the way; and prepare the way of the Lord – the highway for our God.

What if you got a phone call in your home saying that the President of the United States and the First Lady were going to be having dinner with you this Thursday at 5:30 p.m.? I imagine between now and Thursday at 5:30 p.m., you would be a very busy person! You would want to make sure everything in your home was just right, and you and all of your family members were ready to receive the President and the First Lady. The meaning you got from the phone call is the same meaning that is conveyed in the passage from Isaiah 40 – get

> But the angel said to him, "Do not be afraid, Zacharias, for your prayer is heard; and your wife Elizabeth will bear you a son, and you shall call his name John. And you will have joy and gladness, and many will rejoice at his birth. For he will be great in the sight of the Lord, and shall drink neither wine nor strong drink. He will also be filled with the Holy Spirit, even from his mother's womb. And he will turn many of the children of Israel to the Lord their God. He will also go before Him in the spirit and power of Elijah, 'to turn the hearts of the fathers to the children,' and the disobedient to the wisdom of the just, to make ready a people prepared for the Lord." *Luke 1:13-17*

everything ready. He is coming. He is on the way.

The Prophesied Forerunner

In the New Testament, the greatest example of a person carrying the forerunner anointing other than Jesus is John the Baptist. John the Baptist announced and gave forewarning to the people that the Savior was on the way. That certainly was the decree that was given to John the Baptist as a herald, announcing the first coming of Jesus. We find out in chapter one of Luke that John the Baptist was the one who was to carry this forerunner anointing – to announce and to prepare the people for the coming of the King.

> **Herald**
> A messenger, a bearer of news, a precursor.

The angel appeared to Zacharias in the temple and told him that his wife Elizabeth would have a son. Through this angel, the Lord tells them who John is going to be. He will live a consecrated life. He will be filled with the Holy Spirit from his mother's womb. He will turn many of the children of Israel to the Lord their God. He will also go before Him in the spirit and power of Elijah to turn the hearts of the fathers to the children and the disobedient to the wisdom of the just, to make ready a people prepared for the Lord.

We need to realize how involved God is in the lives of His people! About 33 years before Jesus would come into the streets and be hailed as Hosanna, the son of David, God blessed the couple Zacharias and Elizabeth with a child who became John the Baptizer who was filled with the Holy Spirit from his mother's womb!

In other words, God began preparing the preparer John years and years ahead of time. Sometimes we get discouraged. We may think, "When is it going to happen? I thought God called me. I thought I had a call. I thought doors would open." Understand that God works through time to prepare those He is calling to prepare His people for His

17

arrival.ᵠ God prepares the preparers, and then the preparers prepare the people.

The Next Visitation

The concept of a forerunner anointing refers to God preparing people and raising them up to prepare His people for the next visitation of God. Now certainly that is going to be true as we are prepared for the second coming of Christ, but I believe it is also true that there is a release of this forerunner anointing on individuals, and even on congregations, who are called by the Lord to prepare their city, to prepare their community, to prepare their region, and to prepare their nation for the next visitation of God.

> Then He said to them, "The harvest truly is great, but the laborers are few; therefore pray the Lord of the harvest to send out laborers into His harvest. Go your way; behold, I send you out as lambs among wolves.
> Matthew 9: 37-38

God often moves in this way – to prepare people and then release them to prepare people. Chapter nine of Matthew tells us that prayers of intercession precede the release of the forerunner anointing. Prayer brings in the workers who bring in the harvest. Zacharias prayed and ministered before the Lord and received the revelation that he would have a son who would herald the coming of the Messiah. God wants to release the mantle of the anointing on you. If you already carry the mantle, then God wants to give you spiritual understanding of how it is to operate in your life and how it is to be expressed in your ministry.

Be Ready for Rejection

Not everyone receives the ministry of the forerunner. Not everyone is ready when a visitation of God arrives. When John the Baptist declared, "Prepare ye the way of the Lord," he had a message of repentance. What happened? Many of the people refused to prepare.

ᵠ *Have you ever felt frustrated because you feel that God is not working as fast as you would like in your life? What can you ask of the Lord to help your heart be at rest with His timing? Why don't you ask Him for it right now?*

John, Chapter One, says of Jesus, "He came unto His own, and his own did not receive Him." He was rejected. Jesus Himself, out of His own heart, said, "Jerusalem, Jerusalem, how often I have wanted to gather you together as a hen does her chicks, but you would not." Why did the people not receive the ministry of the forerunner?

Those who received and recognized the ministry of John the Baptizer and who had hearts broken by repentance were prepared to receive the ministry of Jesus when He came on the scene. All John had to do was to say, "Behold the Lamb of God, who takes away the sin of the world," and his disciples went to follow Jesus.

The ministry of the forerunner is to prepare the people to recognize and follow the Spirit's next visitation so that they will be ready to go on with God. They will not be like the Scribes, the Sadducees and the Pharisees, who stood face to face with Jesus and never knew he was God. The idea of forerunner anointing ministry is very vital and important for us in the season in which we are living. We need to be preparing people for the second coming of Christ.

Remember that Luke Chapter One prophetically says of John the Baptist that he would operate in the spirit and the power of Elijah. In other words, John the Baptist, would be a voice declaring the word of the Lord from the wilderness, having an anointing on his life that would be the same anointing that was on the prophet Elijah's life. It is important that we understand the nature of the spirit and power of Elijah because that is the same anointing that is on the forerunner.

The Spirit of Elijah

Elijah was the prophet of God in the Old Testament – a spokesperson of God. He carried such an anointing and such a mantle that he could stand before the Earthly king of his day, Ahab, and declare, "It will not rain except by my

And Elijah the Tishbite, of the inhabitants of Gilead, said to Ahab, "As the Lord God of Israel lives, before whom I stand, there shall not be dew nor rain these years, except at my word." 1 Kings 17:1

word." That is authority, and that is power! That is the kind of anointing and authority that can be carried by someone who has the forerunner anointing on their life.

Satan rises up against someone with the forerunner anointing. Ahab and Jezebel tried to kill Elijah. Their nation was in a drought, people were dying because of famine, and they wanted to kill and silence the voice of the only person who had the authority to call for it to rain again! Satan, through the power of deception and bondage, can cause people to rise up and stand against the very thing they need for their survival. That is happening in America right now. But there is going to be an increase in the amount of forerunner anointing poured out upon people as the authority, the spirit, and the power of Elijah is bestowed upon those called and desiring to receive it.

God raised up Elijah to be His prophetic voice and carry the forerunner anointing, and it brought restoration into the land. Elijah stood before 450 prophets of the Baal – 400 prophets of the grove. He called down fire from heaven, and they saw restoration and revival in Israel. When God begins to move to fulfill His purposes, it is called *kairos*, that season of refreshing during the opportune time of God. He'll work years and years and years and years up to that moment, but when kairos comes, there is an inundation of the power of God to fulfill His mandates in the Earth.

Elijah said to Elisha, "Ask! What may I do for you, before I am taken away from you?" Elisha said, "Please let a double portion of your spirit be upon me." So he said, "You have asked a hard thing. Nevertheless, if you see me when I am taken from you, it shall be so for you; but if not, it shall not be so." Then it happened, as they continued on and talked, that suddenly a chariot of fire appeared with horses of fire, and separated the two of them; and Elijah went up by a whirlwind into Heaven. II Kings 2:9-11

A Personal Prayer

Father, prepare my heart for what you have prepared for me. Help my life to be an influence for good in your kingdom. Lord I recognize that I am in a season of preparation and you know what I need. Help me to have the humility of heart to receive from your hand what I truly need. Forgive me for the times I have tried to instruct others without heeding the same instruction for my life. I do not want to miss what you are doing now. I do not want to live in the land of "has been" or sit on the sidelines disqualified. I want to be like you Lord Jesus. I want my heart to be constantly filled with the joy, hope, and expectancy of your return. May your mercy cover me, and may your grace prepare me for the process of preparation. I love you and bless your name, Lord Jesus.

Chapter Two

Forerunners Are Restorers

Elijah was the restorer in his day. Through him the Lord restored Israel, destroyed the prophets of Baal and the prophets of the grove, called down fire from Heaven, and ultimately, Jezebel herself was dealt the deathblow. Who was Elijah's protégé and spiritual son? Elijah's mantle fell on Elisha, who because of his commitment to Elijah ,the forerunner, received a double portion of the anointing. You can count the miracles recorded in Scripture that Elijah was used of God to perform, and the number of miracles that Elisha performed in Scripture is twice the number that Elijah performed. Elisha carried a double portion. Why? He was Elijah's spiritual son.

Double Portion
A generous amount of a whole, implying special favor toward the recipient.

Because Elisha committed himself to the purposes of Elijah and submitted to the mantle that Elijah carried, God honored that submission. After the time of preparation under Elijah's covering when Elijah was taken up to Heaven, Elisha received the anointing times two.

It is very important to understand the role of submission and yielding to the forerunners who God has placed over you because it will give exponential increase to the anointing that is in your life. We will study this in greater detail later on in this book.

John the Baptist carried the spirit of Elijah at the first coming of Jesus, and there will be a generation that will carry the anointing of the Spirit of Elijah before the Second Coming of Jesus Christ. This kind of anointing is poured out during times of restoration.

The anointing that was carried by Elijah is the same anointing that was carried by John the Baptizer. John worked in the spirit and the power of Elijah. He had such an anointing that people kept asking, "John, are you the One? Are you the One?" But he always pointed them to Jesus. He had the forerunner anointing, yet he knew he was just a preparer.

Five-Fold Forerunners

Those people who operate in one of the five-fold ministries of the church have an anointing parallel to the forerunner anointing. Such an anointing is given to the body to equip or to prepare the saints to do the works of ministry. There is a sense in which anyone operating in a five-fold ministry gift is to operate under the forerunner anointing – the preparer's anointing. They are equipped to prepare people for the move of God, to be sensitive to the Spirit of God, to move when God moves, and to recognize the activity of God.

The disciples of Jesus, when they were sent out by Jesus, had the forerunner anointing on them, even before the cross. Jesus, in His own ministry here on the Earth, sent teams of two ahead of Him to prepare the people for His arrival. He told His disciples to go into the cities and announce, "The Kingdom of Heaven is at hand. The Kingdom of God is here." The Messenger, the Redeemer sent to the Earth, and the forerunner knows that what he or she is called to do is to prepare the people to meet the Lord and declare that the Lord is at hand. Q2

> After these things the Lord appointed seventy others also, and sent them two by two before His face into every city and place where He Himself was about to go.
> Luke 10:1
>
> ...say to them 'The kingdom of God has come near to you.'
> Luke 10:9

Forerunners Then — Forerunners Now

Not only do we see this forerunner anointing operating in the Old Testament and in the New Testament, but prophetically, the spirit of Elijah and power of Elijah are also operating now. In other words, there is a futuristic element to it.

> Shekinah (Hebrew)
> From the root 'to dwell' that is translated as the glorious 'Presence' of God.

Chapter 17 of Matthew describes the transfiguration. Jesus took three of the disciples up onto a mountain, where He

---

Q2 Can you name another person in the Bible who has characteristics of the forerunner anointing? What characteristics of the forerunner anointing do they have?

23

was transfigured and began to shine like the sun! What was it that made him shine? It was the shekinah glory of God. God unzipped him a little bit, and let the shekinah that was always resident within him spill out. What happened when the disciples saw the glory? They hit the dust! When the glory of God is manifest, it can cause us to collapse. We are made from dust, and when we see the glory, we realize, "Man, I just need to go back to the dust. God is God, and I am dirt." When God's glory is manifested to us in that powerful way, we do what the disciples did; we hit the ground. When the glory really manifests, people find themselves on their faces bowing in the presence of an awesome holy God. Adam's first moment of awareness was experienced in the glorious presence of God. We are made for this, and ultimately the restoration of all things will result in our spending an eternity in God's glorious presence.

Now, it is interesting that Chapter 40 of Isaiah tells us that Isaiah was to prepare the people for the glory of the Lord to be revealed. The whole Earth is groaning for the manifestation of the glory of God in the sons and daughters of God on the Earth.

> The glory of the Lord shall be revealed, And all flesh shall see it together.
> Isaiah 40:5

When God created Adam and Eve, He wanted children of the Earth to manifest His glory and to be fruitful, multiply, and fill the Earth. There is going to be a time in the middle of gross darkness when the glory of the Lord will be manifested in His children on the Earth and His brightness will be seen.

Prior to that marvelous time is the time of the ministry of the forerunner, preparing the people to get ready for the revelation, the unveiling, the revealing, the appearing, the revelation of Jesus Christ coming back. Jesus, as the last Adam, will bring things back into order as they were in the beginning on this Earth that was cursed by sin. His glory will cover the face of the Earth.

Who had the disciples seen with Jesus at the transfiguration? Moses and Elijah appeared with Jesus; Moses representing the law of God, the written word, and Elijah representing the prophet of God, the spoken word. They were there with Jesus, who is the Logos, the eternal living Word of God. In that one glorious revelation and visitation from God on the mount, we have a picture of the written word, the spoken word, and the living Word being together in a defining moment.

On one occasion, his disciples asked Him, "Why, then, do the Scribes say that Elijah must come first?"

Jesus is talking about John the Baptist when He tells his disciples that Elijah has come already, and that the people did not know him but did to him whatever they wished. Jesus understood that the anointing on John the Baptist's life was the spirit and power of Elijah and that the people did not recognize John the Baptist as Elijah. In other words, many did not receive John the Baptist, and many would not receive Jesus.

> **Logos** (Greek)
> A name for the Living Word, Jesus Christ, who is the personal expression of the thoughts of God to man. It means word or reason.

The Restoration of All Things

We know that all things will be restored before Jesus returns because we are told so in Chapter Three of Acts. This is one of the most important Scriptures that help us understand the events that are taking place during the days in which we are living. Jesus had already come, been crucified, been buried, had risen from the grave, and ascended to the Father. The Church then began preaching the message of his return to the earth. It is absolutely vital to understand Acts 3:21. Peter tells us that since the beginning of time God has spoken through the prophets about restoration.

> *Repent therefore and be converted, that your sins may be blotted out, so that times of refreshing may come from the presence of the Lord, and that He may send Jesus Christ, who was preached to you before,* **whom Heaven must receive until the times of restoration of all things***, which God has spoken by the mouth of all His holy prophets since the world began.*
> *Acts 3:19-21*
> (Emphasis added)

Peter taught that Heaven will receive Jesus until the restoration of all things. Understand what is said here. If God said it is going to happen, it is going to happen. He revealed it to His prophets. They, under the

25

forerunner anointing, began to declare to the people, "This is what God is going to do."

Peter tells us very clearly that "Heaven must receive Jesus until....". He is not coming back until the restoration of all things. "Must" carries the idea of absolute moral necessity. In order for God to be a God of His word, heaven must receive Jesus until, that is always a time word in Scripture, a point of time that God moves to action until the restoration of all things. Not some things, but the restoration of *all* things.

Now what does that tell us? Jesus is not coming back until the restoration of all things. In other words, before His second coming glory to establish His rule and reign on the Earth, there will be a major shifting of all things into proper alignment so that the Earth will be ready for the visitation of the King of Kings in second coming glory. In order for this to be established, there is going to be harvest, and there is going to be judgment. There is going to be a great move of God in mercy and there is going to be a great move of God in wrath.

Jesus clearly taught and preached that the spirit of Elijah would be present to bring about restoration. We know we are living close to the days that Jesus is coming back. We know the Scripture says Elijah must first come to restore all things. Therefore, if we know that this has to happen before Jesus returns, then we should be looking for the release of the spirit of Elijah and the power of Elijah on the people of God in order to prepare this Earth and prepare the bride. That is what its all about, preparing the people of God and enlarging the camp of the people of God. We are close to His coming in these days, so therefore, we should be sensing through his Spirit the releasing of the spirit of Elijah and power of Elijah on the church and onto people who are carrying the forerunner mantle.

Awaiting the Spirit of Elijah

I once read that in the Jewish and Messianic Jewish celebration of the Passover, there are four cups. Some have to do with redemption and suffering, but there is also the cup of Elijah. In the celebration of

Passover, before it is over, the celebrants will take the cup of Elijah, and they will pray for the spirit of Elijah to come upon them to prepare them for the coming, or in a Messianic version, the second coming of the King. May the mantle of Elijah fall upon our generation, and may we pick it up and smite the Jordan in front of us and watch it part in response to prophetic power and anointing!

Here's a synopsis for the sake of clarity:

* John the Baptist operated in the Spirit and power of Elijah to herald in the first coming of Jesus. Luke 1:17, Matthew 11:14

*Elijah appeared and talked with Jesus at the transfiguration. Matthew 17:3

*Some thought Jesus was Elijah. Some thought he was calling for Elijah from the cross. The people clearly were looking for Elijah to be associated with the establishment of Messiah's kingdom. Matthew 16:14, Mark 15:35

*Jesus taught that when Elijah comes, he will restore all things. Matthew 17:10-12

*Peter preaching after the ascension declared that Heaven would receive Jesus until the restoration of all things. Acts 3:19-21

*Therefore, the Spirit and power of Elijah, that is to restore all things, will be operative prior to the second coming of Jesus which will occur commensurate with the restoration of all things.

A Personal Prayer

Dear Heavenly Father, I thank you that the times and seasons are in your hands. I thank you that my life is in your hands. I ask you to restore my soul. Bring all the needed restoration into my heart and life so that I can be a proclaimer of restoration to others. I have confidence that you will ultimately restore all things. I pray for sensitivity to what you want to do in the lives of the people around me as well. I ask for Heaven's best to flow into their lives. I desire to operate in the Spirit and power of Elijah to whatever degree is possible for my life. Use me for your eternal purposes. I bless your name. In Jesus name, amen.

Chapter Three

Leaping for the Lord

If you carry forerunner anointing, there is one thing that you will notice. When the presence of God manifests, you will want to leap. Well, at least you will be stirred up on the inside. How it manifests may vary in your life. Read on and you will understand what I am talking about. The forerunner has a sensitivity to the nearness of the Lord. Prophetically speaking, the forerunner will have a sensitivity to the coming of the Lord. Practically speaking, as a forerunner, you will have a spiritual sensitivity when the Lord is present and when the Lord is about to do something. You may not know all the specifics of what is about to happen, but your "forerunometer" will be responding. Forerunometer? What's that? Well, I guess I'm forerunning a new term. Patronize me and stay with me, okay?

The forerunner anointing recognizes the nearness of the Lord. In Luke Chapter 1 the angel appeared to Zacharias and told him that he and Elizabeth would have a son, and his name would be called John. The angel of the Lord had also appeared to Mary and told her that the Holy Spirit would overshadow her, and she would carry the seed of God. Mary and Elizabeth were cousins, and both were having supernatural phenomenon surrounding their pregnancies. Zacharias and Elizabeth were past their prime to say

> *And behold, you will conceive in your womb and bring forth a Son, and shall call His name JESUS. He will be great, and will be called the Son of the Highest; and the Lord God will give Him the throne of His father David.*
> *Luke 1: 31-32*

the least, and they received angelic visitation with an announcement about a son who would be born to them. About six months into her pregnancy, her cousin Mary had an incredible visitation from God. A little virgin girl who had never known a man is told by God that there will be a creative, miraculous act of God generated inside her womb. She is told that she is going to give birth to God's own son. Angelic activity announced it, and it was carried out by the creative work of the

Holy Spirit who planted the promised Seed of God inside her womb. Talk about forerunning!

The Word and the Spirit

In the beginning of the Bible we find the Holy Spirit hovering and God speaking, and the result we see there is the release of dynamic, creative, and miraculous power. Similarly, the Holy Spirit hovered over Mary's life in response to what God had spoken and the spoken word becomes the living Word in the Christ Child, and then you see the miraculous activity of God through His life. God is amazing, isn't He?

With this almost unbelievable news in hand and a child in her womb, Mary traveled to see her cousin, Elizabeth. The Bible says she went to the hill country with haste. With haste! You might be inclined to do that too, if you have never known a man and found out you were pregnant! Upon her arrival, something astounding happens that gives some indication about the special relationship that these unborn babes are going to enjoy in their future destinies. When Elizabeth heard the greeting of Mary, the babe in her womb leaped. Elizabeth's baby leaped in her womb! Who's that? It's John the baptizer-to-be. When little baby John hears the greeting of Mary, he leaps in his momma's womb. When he jumped, Elizabeth, his mother, was filled with the Holy Spirit. Don't tell me this baby is not anointed! God was preparing the preparer. When God begins cultivating that seed of destiny He has inside of you, you will be stirred as well. You will be stirred, motivated and influenced by others who are carrying something similar. This is what is happening with these two powerful women of God who are carrying destiny in their wombs.

> *And it happened, when Elizabeth heard the greeting of Mary, that the babe leaped in her womb; and Elizabeth was filled with the Holy Spirit. Then she spoke out with a loud voice and said, "Blessed are you among women, and blessed is the fruit of your womb! But why is this granted to me, that the mother of my Lord should come to me? For indeed, as soon as the voice of your greeting sounded in my ears, the babe leaped in my womb for joy. Blessed is she who believed, for there will be a fulfillment of those things which were told her from the Lord."*
> Luke 1:41-45

30

Speaking + Hearing = Birthing

It may be that when baby John resting in Elizabeth's womb heard the voice of the mother of the Lord, that at that moment, he was filled with the Spirit. Or, it may mean that at the very moment of conception, he carried the anointing of the Holy Spirit on his life. But this we know, when he heard Mary speak, he did cartwheels! John expressed his gleeful excitement of being in the proximity of the Anointed One Himself—Jesus. Years later, you see this same excitement in John on an occasion when Jesus walks by and John points him out to his disciples and tells them, "He must increase, I must decrease. You need to follow him now. He's going to take away the sins of the world. I am not worthy to unlatch his sandals. He's got the Holy Ghost on him and the fire of God." This recognition of Jesus began while John was still in his mother's womb. It must always be a part of the person who has been chosen to forerun. The inability to discern the Lord's presence can result in a person cutting a new path in the wrong direction. When John jumped, his momma got an impartation too!

Elizabeth knew something was up. She was compelled to speak a word of blessing to Mary. There are some dynamic things happening here. Get this picture. Here is Elizabeth; she is carrying a baby. The baby's filled with the Holy Spirit. Here comes Mary; she has been visited by the Holy Spirit and is carrying the Christ Child in her womb. Mary greets Elizabeth, and when the greeting entered Elizabeth's ear, something happened in her womb.

Both Elizabeth and Mary were in the place they were in because of a word from the Lord that had been released and received into their lives in spite of the impossibilities of their natural circumstances. The word was not confined by the natural. Mary had responded to the Lord's word by saying "Be it done unto me according to your word (Luke 1:38)." You see, when you start hearing the voice of the Lord, something ought to start happening in your womb. When God starts speaking, it should start birthing things in your life. Elizabeth hears the voice of the mother of her Lord in her ear, the baby in her womb picks up on the nearness of the Lord and leaps!

31

Your DNA Contains Destiny

You know what this tells us? When you operate in the Spirit, it has nothing to do with how developed you are in the natural. This baby John could not yet walk. This baby could not yet talk. This baby was not even fully developed. He does not even know how to spell. He can't add 2 + 2. He does not know how to speak. He does not know history. But do you know what? He does know his destiny! His little receiver in his Spirit already understands the Holy Spirit inside of him and is already recognizing the nearness of the Lord and already propelling him toward his God ordained destiny. Destiny is something released in your spirit. There will be times in your life when the Spirit without your knowledge in the natural is positioning you to be where you need to be, to get what you need to get in order to see what you need to see, so that you can be who you were made to be. This is the fulfillment of destiny. Dear forerunner, in reality, it's already in your DNA. Let it out! One of the things that releases the destiny that you carry is the reception of the word of the Lord. The "word" which carries the life of God will impregnate your DNA and release all the things that God has ordained to be inside of you. The word and the Spirit will combine to create, develop, and birth in your life the destiny and purposes of God for you. Let the Spirit take you whitersoever he wills. If you've already been there and have all the answers, you're not forerunning.

Do not be intimidated that you may not have a bunch of degrees hanging on your wall. It is not about who you are in the natural. It's about what you're carrying in the spirit. This six-month-old baby in the womb is in the process of development, yet he has sensitivity to the nearness of the Lord. He responds to the nearness of the Lord and leaps. Do you know what his response does? Because he responds in his little spirit to the proximity of the Lord by leaping, it sends a Holy Ghost jolt through his momma.

> Sometimes in a worship service when the presence of the Lord begins to manifest, all of a sudden, all over the house, you see people on their face and you see people dancing before the Lord. What is happening? The people are sensing the presence of the Lord, and they are responding.

32

She gets filled with the Holy Spirit. It was one small leap for a babe that heralded one giant blessing for all mankind. Don't underestimate the baby steps that you have to take during the process of development of God's call on your life. By the way, no matter how long you have been forerunning, there will always be baby steps on each new adventure that God leads you into. When you learn to be sensitive and you start responding to the nearness of the Lord, it begins to impact, influence, and affect the people around you.

Let the Prophetic Kick in

Little John, six months along in development, did not know protocol and tact and the customs of the church. He just got busy recognizing that Jesus was present! He started leaping and his mother was filled with the Holy Spirit. Not only that, when the Holy Spirit hit Elizabeth, the manifestation of the forerunner anointing began operating in her life, and she began prophesying. She received a word of knowledge that Mary was carrying the Lord in her womb. Nobody had told her, and there was a release of the prophetic. Imagine how encouraging it was for Mary to hear this prophetic word. She understood why she had been led to spend time with Elizabeth because she would be with someone else who believed her story. Often a word of prophecy will affirm the identity of what you are carrying in the spirit and it gives you confidence that you are in the right place at the right time.

A Prophecy to the Nations

I remember in the summer of 1999 after I had stepped away from the pastorate to minister to the wider body of Christ. I really did not fully understand what I was supposed to do. The Lord had told me to "step out", and I did. My wife, four children, and I stepped away from all visible means of support having no home to live in, no insurance, and no knowledge of what would be next. This was quite a change from pastoring a large church, living in a big brick house with a large salary that included a membership at the local country club. I just knew I was supposed to minister in the area of unity in the body of Christ, healing, and the restoration of spiritual power in the Church.

It was amazing at the string of miracles that the Lord tied together to position us for our destiny during those days. There are so many powerful stories that I could share. I do want to share one that fits in the flow of what I am teaching in this chapter. I had been asked to speak at a conference in Birmingham, Alabama at Advocate Ministries where Bill French, one of my spiritual fathers, ministered. In this same conference was a dear lady from Chicago who was ministering in the area of the prophetic. During one of her sessions, she called me out and began prophesying over me. All of this was still very new to me at the time, but it was so powerful. She prophesied about apostolic ministry and traveling to the nations and impacting the nations. This was so different than what I was experiencing in the natural at the time. Then she got really specific and mentioned traveling to Africa, Eastern Europe, Central America and told me that she did not see anything in the Far East. She said that my way would be paid for. She mentioned that my family would be given a nice place to live while I was away. She did not know the details of my situation at the time or that my family had just moved into a new dream house. This is another whole series of miracles. She stated that the Lord was going to establish my ministry to the nations.

Within a year, I was contacted to travel to Africa on a preaching trip, and my expenses were provided. I was also contacted with an invitation to travel to the Ukraine and minister to all the SBC missionaries in that country, as well as minister a week in their seminary. My trip and expenses were provided. Shortly after that, I ended up in India and had to leave the country early being pursued by the police under threat of arrest by the police for preaching the Gospel. I should have listened a little closer, huh? The next month, I was in Honduras seeing God move in powerful ways. It was amazing how quickly things transitioned to the nations. In a period of seven months, I had set foot in nine different nations. Then, just as quickly, the Lord thrust me into the congregation that I am now pastoring,and we have been able to see multiplication in the area of impacting the nations. As a matter of fact, the nations are at the heart of the vision that the Lord has given us as a congregation.

During this season of preparation and positioning, there were many challenges, many miracles, and many lessons learned. But God was faithful to encourage us along the way through words released into us by other forerunners. We are always in a season of "something". Sometimes in the middle of the season of something, we see nothing. During these times, the glimpses that the Lord releases to us through the prophetic are especially powerful and meaningful. These words cause a stirring of faith inside of us that tells us that more is happening that we can see and know in the natural. God has not forgotten us, and He is preparing and positioning us for destiny. When these words are declared over us, we feel a little like Mary did when Elizabeth prophesied that God was doing something special in her life.

Leaping Prepares You to Jump Hurdles

It is important we understand that the operation of the spirit of Elijah will be protested. Leaping in the womb just prepares our muscles to clear the hurdles that will confront us a little farther around the track. There will be opposition because wherever you see the spirit of Elijah, there is the counterpart of Satan, the spirit of Jezebel, to suffocate, stifle, and kill the prophetic voice. Religion will want to shut down the forerunner anointing. Jezebel will want to sever it and bring it to an end. But in its innocence and purity before the Lord, it releases great joy. It causes people to know something is happening. People feel it reverberating deep inside of them, and they realize that it is what they were made for. They understand they are headed somewhere, and they do not even know where yet, but they know it is going to be good. When the forerunner anointing operates, it starts to stir all those feelings up in people, and then they start stepping into the flow. Then they get under the influence of the anointing, and they start prophesying. They start influencing and impacting the people around them. Next thing you know, everybody in town is coming out, just like they did to see John the Baptist, all the region gathered around to hear what he had to say. It is the forerunner anointing. It is the spirit and power of Elijah, and for you, I believe it is going to be twofold, a double portion.

God is raising up forerunners in our day to announce the next visitation of God. I am an optimist and I believe in the Word. God has an awakening that's going to hit this world, and He is working right now to raise up people to begin to declare the word of the Lord so that people will be prepared to receive it.

It is all about HIM! The forerunner runs ahead and tells the people, "Look at Jesus, he is coming. He is coming!" God is moving and working. Maybe you are the next one He wants to touch. I believe you are because that is His heart – to touch hurting people, to touch hungry people. Maybe you are just carrying a burden that's more than you can bear. You have tripped over a hurdle or two and you are battling discouragement and thinking of turning in your shoes. There is an anointing to bear that burden. Do not struggle if the Lord is dealing with you. Do not struggle. Just submit; lay the pride aside and say, "Have your way, Lord. Whatever you require of me, Lord, I will do it. Have your way." He even uses missed hurdles to teach us to be better runners.

> It is all about Jesus. He died for you. He is the One that is going to heal your sick body. He is the One that is going to save you from the path of destruction. He is the One that is going to set you free. He is the One you were made to serve. He is the One Who is coming back to rule and reign over the earth.

Do you want the forerunner anointing? Do you want to operate in it? Fall on your knees and ask God to activate it in your life.

A Personal Prayer

Father God, right now I honor Jesus. I want to be a forerunner pointing to Jesus. Lord, you said that Elijah must first come to restore all things, and you said you would come then after that. Lord, I would ask right now that you would prepare my heart so that you could trust me with a forerunner anointing. Lord, I really believe in my spirit that you have called me to carry the forerunner anointing.

36

Lord, help me to realize the importance of responding to your call. I ask for the release of the spirit and power of the forerunner to be upon me. I pray, sweet Holy Spirit, that you would begin to reveal to me what rough places need to be made smooth in my life, what mountains need to be overcome in my life, what valleys need to be walked through in my life, because Lord, I know you have to lead me through all that before I can stand before others and tell them to make the rough ways smooth and the mountains low and the valleys high.

I welcome your ministry, Holy Spirit. Begin revealing sin, putting your finger on those things that would cause me to be hypocritical, to be religious, and to operate with the spirit of Jezebel and control. Lord, prepare me to be a preparer, so that I can prepare others to be with you.

I thank you, Lord Jesus, and I bless your name. In the name of the Forerunner of all Forerunners, Jesus, amen!

Chapter Four

Obscure People from Obscure Places

Have you ever thought, "How could God use me? I am just a nobody from a small town that no one has ever heard of." "No one will listen to me. I don't have all the degrees. I've hardly been outside my own county."

No one had heard much of Nazareth either. Bethlehem was just an obscure little village. A ministry based in the wilderness, the wild place, is more than a little puzzling as well. Chapter 3 of Matthew tells us that the ministry of John the Baptist took place in the wilderness of Judea. It was not long after that voice began

> *In those days John the Baptist came preaching in the wilderness of Judea, and saying, "Repent, for the kingdom of Heaven is at hand!" For this is he who was spoken of by the prophet Isaiah, saying: "The voice of one crying in the wilderness: 'Prepare the way of the Lord; Make His paths straight.'" Matthew 3:1-3*

crying out in the wilderness until the entire region became impacted by John's message. Out of the hidden place, John was thrust into the middle of history. It is in the hidden places that God prepares his forerunners.

Making Somebodies out of Nobodies

The forerunner anointing often comes upon obscure people from obscure places. Where was Jesus born? He was born in Bethlehem, and what does the Scripture say about that? If you were going to chart a course and make a plan for the King of Kings to make His entrance in the Earth, you would probably choose some big, first class, cutting edge city to usher in His arrival. But God chose a little obscure town called Bethlehem. It was the shepherds out in the fields away from the crowds who were called to see Him that

> *But you, Bethlehem Ephrathah, Though you are little among the thousands of Judah, Yet out of you shall come forth to Me The One to be Ruler in Israel, Whose goings forth are from of old, From everlasting." Micah 5: 2*

night.Q It was their voices that came crying from the out of the way place announcing the good news.

God puts His hand on somebody. Nobody even knows who they are. Nobody has ever even heard of them. The person is from a place that you have to locate on a map that zooms in on *every* little town! Scripture tells us that God chooses the foolish things of this world to confound the wise. Remember, John the Baptist was not your normal, everyday kind of guy. John the Baptist did not look like everybody else, did not dress like everybody else, and had a diet a *little bit* different than everybody else. He was an obscure person. He lived a consecrated life. John was a voice crying in the wilderness. John arose to be who God ordained him to be even though it was unorthodox and different. In the Old Testament account of Israel's journey toward Canaan, they were stopped because they saw giants and viewed themselves as grasshoppers. John was not stopped because of the culture he was stepping into; he ate grasshoppers. He knew he was called. He had courage and determination to fulfill that call on his life. The Holy Spirit would be his helper even though he would not know the depths of the kingdom and the Spirit that those who would follow him would come to know. He was willing to announce that which he had not yet seen. He truly was a prophet and more than a prophet. It takes a selfless person to become a true forerunner. You have to be willing to bleed so that others won't have to; isn't this what Jesus did? Isn't this what John did? Isn't this what Paul did? It will also be true for each of us. This is why the preparation is so important. This may give us insight as to why the obscure person from an obscure place is suited for forerunning. They are not used to getting the credit because they have seldom been recognized. They know what it is like to have to wait and wait and wait. They are not used to hearing about who they are and where they are from. They are just serving Jesus in the hidden places until one day

---

Q *Has the Lord ever spoken to you through someone from an out of the way place?*

things shift, and they are called to expand their territory and enlarge the borders of their ministry.

Nowheres that become Somewheres

God often chooses to visit obscure places. The Smithton Outpouring 'Revival in the Cornfield' started in 1996 in a little white church out in the middle of a Missouri cornfield with just a few people. It got so big it had to be moved to Kansas City, and people from all over the world have come there and still do. Then there is that sidewalk church near an airport in Toronto. Toronto is a big place, but at the airport is an out of the way church that God chose to visit. Since 1994, God has been powerfully moving at Toronto Airport Christian Fellowship. Pensacola, Florida is not necessarily the biggest place, but God moved powerfully there at the Brownsville Assembly of God starting in 1995 and is still at work there today.

Back at the turn of the century, there was an obscure black brother who had one eye named William Seymour. He was not even allowed to sit in class at Bible school. He had to sit out in the hall and overhear the lectures. The school would not let him attend classes because he was the wrong color. But God chose him. God chose *him* to be the carrier of an anointing that would herald a Pentecost-like revival to occur on planet Earth called the "Azusa Street Revival." People around the world today, a 100 years later, still mention the name "William Seymour." What about the young teenager name Evan Roberts who also became an international household name because of the way the Lord used him in the 1904 Welch Revival. Billy Graham was told that he would never make a preacher. A pretty pathetic prediction considering he is respected around the world as *the* Evangelist—the preacher of the Gospel. It's not about where you start; it's about where God can take you if you are willing to prepare and make the trip.

God historically has worked powerfully choosing obscure people from obscure places, raising them up, and using them as point persons to herald His next visitation. Sometimes, He does it with the least expected. Who would have thought that God would use an Episcopalian priest named Dennis Bennett as a forerunner to carry a mantle, an anointing, to birth the charismatic movement that would cause many Evangelical churches to open their arms and receive the fullness of the Holy Spirit and the operation of the gifts of the Holy Spirit in their lives and in their midst?

Forerunners Training Forerunners

God is also raising up forerunners to forerun the training of forerunners. One of these forerunners of forerunners is Mike Bickle. Mike will tell you that he is just an ordinary guy. God used him to birth a movement of intercession and prayer that has drawn people from around the world to Kansas City, Missouri, and has sent people from Kansas City, Missouri to nations around the world. God moved upon Mike's heart to start extended times of prayer in the church he was pastoring several years ago. Since that time a lot has changed in Mike's ministry. God has promoted him from obscurity to a place of honor among his people. For the past five years, there has been a 24 hours a day, seven days a week, uninterrupted flow of intercession, prophetic prayer and worship that has ascended to the heart of the Bridegroom from the International House of Prayer in Kansas City, Missouri. Meeting there around the clock are obscure people from obscure places all around the earth. It is truly an amazing place where forerunners gather to be equipped to prepare for the coming of the Bridegroom for his bride. It has even touched our family deeply because our daughter, Kara Beth, is enrolled there as a student in the Forerunner School of Ministry. She was led by the Lord to a conference there during the same time I was teaching our

> *And Samuel said to Jesse, "The Lord has not chosen these ... Are all the young men here?" Then he said, "There remains yet the youngest, and there he is, keeping the sheep." And Samuel said to Jesse, "Send and bring him. For we will not sit down till he comes here." ... Now he was ruddy, with bright eyes, and good-looking. And the Lord said, "Arise, anoint him; for this is the one!" 1 Samuel 6: 10-12*

congregation about the forerunner anointing. She went through a six-month internship and then into the school of ministry. She is there as I write this book, learning to personally prepare to forerun and to prepare the church for the coming of her Groom and King. This is one place out of many that God is raising up in this hour.

Throughout Scripture are examples of God choosing obscure people to do His work. Remember that little shepherd boy out in the field who had all the other brothers who God did not choose to anoint? God would not put His finger on any of them. God chose a little guy, David, watching sheep out in the field to be His own.

Don't Let Your City Limits Limit You

It is in the wilderness and out of the way places where God will hide you away and prepare you. It is in this place that you must win the battle of who you really are based on what God has put inside of you. If you do not win this personal battle you will not be able to decree the destiny of an entire generation over them. The enemy of your soul wants to hold you back and suppress the call and destiny you carry. He will heap rejection upon you, and you must learn to win this battle. He will unload condemnation on you, and you must win this battle. He will attempt to fasten you where you have always been using the rivets of defeat, but you must also win this battle. With these battles won in the private place, you will be prepared to go public and proclaim to a generation that they, too, have a destiny awaiting them. Where you were born and how you were raised do not have to limit the heights to which you can soar in the Spirit. Do not be limited by what man tells you, because it is the anointing that bears the burden. It is the anointing that breaks the yoke. God is releasing that forerunner anointing in our day, and it often comes upon obscure people from obscure places. You might be the next one God chooses! You may carry the fingerprint of God on your forehead because God has touched you and pointed to you and said, "You are going to be a forerunner, and I am going to use you to break down some walls, make some new wineskins, and usher in my next visitation."

A Personal Prayer

Dear Father, I ask you in the name of Jesus to mold me and shape me into the vessel you want me to be. By an act of faith and the power of the blood of Jesus Christ, I choose right now to break off me the intimidation, fear, doubt, and unbelief that would cause me to view myself as insignificant. You chose where I would be born, who my parents would be, and where I would be raised. I trust that you are using all of this together for my good to prepare me to bring you glory. I submit to you fully. I thank you for who I am and for where I am from. Use me, Lord! I surrender to your purposes for my life. I thank you that there is nothing that can halt the fulfillment of my destiny if I will humble myself under your mighty hand and await your timing. In Jesus name, amen!

Chapter Five

Pioneering the Way

If you are the first one to a new place, you will have to fight the briars, undergrowth, and obstacles that others who follow you will not have to deal with. It was tough for Sir Edmund Hillary to get to the top of Everest, but don't you know it was exhilarating to stand where no other man had ever stood and see what no other man had ever seen! A lot of sacrifice was made by Neil Armstrong to prepare and make it to the moon, but don't you know it was almost intoxicating to leave your footprint on a planet that had never felt the weight of a human being before. We read in Matthew 12 that the Pharisees schemed to destroy Jesus. John had a real harsh word for them. As a matter of fact, he called them "a brood of vipers." We know what happened to John and to Jesus and ultimately to all the disciples. The operation of the forerunner anointing involves sacrifice, persecution and peril. Just read Paul's chronicle of some of the low points of his ministry in 2 Corinthians 11:23-28. The forerunner anointing brings persecution. Paul told young Timothy that living a godly life, in itself, will bring persecution. Living for God in this world is definitely living against the grain.

*Are they ministers of Christ? — I speak as a fool — I am more: in labors more abundant, in stripes above measure, in prisons more frequently, in deaths often. From the Jews five times I received forty stripes minus one. Three times I was beaten with rods; once I was stoned; three times I was shipwrecked; a night and a day I have been in the deep ; in journeys often, in perils of waters, in perils of robbers, in perils of my own countrymen, in perils of the Gentiles, in perils in the city, in perils in the wilderness, in perils in the sea, in perils among false brethren; in weariness and toil, in sleeplessness often, in hunger and thirst, in fastings often, in cold and nakedness — besides the other things, what comes upon me daily: my deep concern for all the churches.
2 Cor 11:23-28*

Q *What are you willing to give up to be a forerunner?*

Being a forerunner means that you, to a certain degree, are a pioneer. An apostle is considered a pioneer. A pioneer is someone who cuts the path so others can follow. Jesus is the Author and Finisher of our faith. That word "author" in the Greek language conveys the idea of somebody blazing a trail, creating a way, cutting a path through the thick places, through the jungle. Jesus was that. As a forerunner, you may be plowing ground that has not been plowed, or you may be leading people from where they are to the place that they need to be for them to be in the middle of what God is doing now. I live in the state of Alabama. The name *Alabama* is from an Indian word which means "thicket clearer." There have been many Alabamians who have blazed trails in various arenas of life. Read through this list of some of the more familiar names and see how many of these Alabamians you recognize:

Alabama (Country Music Band), Hank Aaron, Ralph Abernathy, Tallulah Bankhead, Jimmy Buffett, Hugo Black, George Washington Carver, Nat "King" Cole, Marva Collins (educator), Courteney Cox, The Commodores, Bobby Goldsboro, Fannie Flagg, W. C. Handy, Emmy Lou Harris, Kate Jackson, Sonny James, Dean Jones, Helen Keller, Coretta Scott King, Carl Lewis, George Lindsey, Joe Louis, Willie Mays, Jim Nabors, Jesse Owens, Rosa Parks, Lionel Richie, Jimmie Rodgers, Percy Sledge, Take 6, Toni Tennille, George Wallace, William Weatherford (Red Eagle), Heather Whitestone, Hank Williams, Tammy Wynette, N. Jan Davis (Astronaut), David Satcher (Surgeon General), Bobby Allison, Davey Allison, Charles Barkley, Bobby Bowden, Harvey Glance, Bo Jackson, Willie McCovey, Larry Nelson, Ozzie Newsome, Satchel Paige, Ken Stabler, John Stallworth, Bart Starr Football, Hut Stricklin, Pat Sullivan, and Don Sutton.

We are praying that Alabama would be a place where God raises up many forerunners who would blaze new trails for the Kingdom of God. Even in the secular arena, people from out of the way places can make their mark. How much more can an anointed son or daughter of God impact this world and leave Christ's mark on men, women, boys and girls? But to leave a mark, you have to willing to bear some marks.

As a forerunner willing to cut a path for others, you are going to get marked, cut by the briars, face obstacles and opposition. You are going to get pierced by the thorns. You are going to bear the marks of suffering. God is looking for a people who will visit the highways, the hedges, the thistles, the places where the thorns, briars, and thistles have grown up that have not been visited, and those people will bear the marks of redemption.Q It is like God is saying, "I am looking for people to be forerunners, to go and cut a path through those places that have grown up that have not been visited." This will be true until the gospel has been preached to all the nations. Pioneers are often unappreciated in their own time, but those who follow begin to see the blessing and kingdom benefits of what has been pioneered. If your generation does not recognize the value of the path you have cut for the kingdom, then a future generation will. The heckling that may fill your ears today will be replaced by a "well done my good and faithful servant" at a future time.

You will bear the marks for charting new territory; there will be persecution. Pioneers are always persecuted. Pioneers have to deal with obstacles that other people that come after them do not have to deal with. When God calls you and puts that pioneer spirit on you, or that forerunner anointing on you, you are going to be cut and bruised by the briars and thistles and thorns that mark the path you are cutting for others to follow. The briars vary in their intensity and degree depending upon where you are forerunning and what you have been called to carry. Don't let this discourage you, but neither let it surprise you. There is a cost to be counted. But, being a way maker is worth it all. Paul tells us that those who were saved through his ministry were his crown of rejoicing. All of life involves a measure of pain now for pleasure later, humility now for honor later, and sowing now for harvest later. It is the knowledge that what you are doing is eternal and will result in the changed lives and destinies of people for whom Christ died. In the middle of the briar thicket, there will be battles but the Lord will provide fresh downloads of courage to stay on track if you will just receive.

The Price of Forerunning

> He sent a man before them – Joseph – who was sold as a slave. They hurt his feet with fetters. He was laid in irons. Psalm 105:17-18

Joseph, son of Jacob, received tremendous revelation from God. Psalm 105 tells us that God sent a man before Israel, Joseph. Joseph was a forerunner. When we study his life, we find out that he had to go through many trials before he came into the fullness of his destiny. He underwent many tribulations his brothers did not have to go through so that their nation could be saved. When he stood before his brothers, he told them "And God sent me before you to preserve a posterity for you in the earth, and to save your lives by a great deliverance."

If you are a forerunner, you will pay a price. Not everybody is going to be happy that you want to change things. Not everybody is going to be happy that there is shifting and alignment taking place, that God is setting things in order, that the work of restoration is taking place. Not everybody is going to be happy that it is not business as usual. It is natural for us to be comfortable with what we know and natural for us to fear the unknown. We must shift from the known to the unknown so we can know something more of the ways of God. Isn't this what happens when a person is saved?

Dear reader, when God starts shifting and aligning, if we do not shift, and we do not align with Him, then He will not bless what we are doing. The forerunner anointing enables us to shift when God brings about a shift so that we can be on the cutting edge of what God is doing. I want to be on the cutting edge. I want to be on the front lines. I do not want to read about it in the papers. I do not want to think about, "What would it have been like to have been there?" "What would it be like to see that?" I want to be there. I want to see it. If it means getting cut and bruised and beaten a little bit, so be it. The beating and bruising are part of carrying the forerunner anointing on your life.

You certainly might suffer if your daily life puts you right in the heartbeat of the secular world. You might be in school and surrounded by people who mention God in vulgar expressions. You might be in an office environment, and holiness is not something you get exposed to very much. You might be in a plant or working construction where the atmosphere it is harsh and tough. You may live in a country where it is illegal and life threatening to share your faith in Christ. What God wants is transformation, in the marketplace, in the classroom, in the plants, and on the construction crews and in the nations. God anoints us and gives us the anointing to carry so that He can use us in those environments. He is preparing you to prepare others for Him because He is coming back. When you start being persecuted in your environment, you cannot react with an attitude of superiority. You have to respond to persecution in humility and with a servant's heart so that people will see Christ in you.

John the Baptist was a Forerunner, and Jesus said, "No man born among women is greater than John, but the least in the Kingdom of Heaven is greater than he." As a forerunner, you start seeing what God wants to do before other people are aware of it. But we cannot look at other believers and be superior in our attitudes because God is showing us something He is not showing them.

> You can hear it before they hear it. You can smell it before they smell it. You can taste it before they taste it. You sense it before anybody else is aware of it.

You cannot judge others because they are not seeing, hearing, tasting, smelling, or experiencing what you are. If God has given you an anointing, it is to be used to bring others into what He is doing, and you will not bring them to that place by criticizing, judging, or brow beating. It has to be through serving and humility and expressing the love of Christ and being patient, just like God was with you and me to bring us to the place where we could see, touch, taste, smell it, and experience it.

You were made to love Him. Express it to Him. He is seeking people who will worship Him in spirit and truth and who will pour out all that they have of themselves to know all that they can find in Him.

Take pleasure in your God. Feel His arms of love around you. Let His mercy flood your heart. Away with condemnation! Away with strife! Away with rejection! Away with the spirit of heaviness! Welcome the garments of the Lord upon your life , the garment of praise.

Maybe there is a cry that is now rising up in you. You are thirsty and hungry for more of the Lord. Maybe the call for change and preparation has fallen upon your ears, and you realize there are changes that you need to make. Maybe there is something inside of you saying, "I do not want to be at the back of the line, either. I want to move to the front. I want to be one of those hungry folks. I want to be somebody God can trust to use."

A Personal Prayer

Father God, thank you for your Word. Lord, I want be a forerunner. Lord, I do not want to be bringing up the rear and getting hand me down reports about what You have done. Lord, I do not ask for this out of pride. I ask for it, Lord, because I am hungry. I ask for it because I believe it is available. Release it, Father, in my life. Help me to be willing to pay the price. Help me, Lord, to be used of you to gather people together. Help me, Father, to hear the call for change and preparation so that I can issue the call for change and preparation. Lord, I know that you are going to prepare me before I can prepare others. Help me to receive from you.

Chapter Six

Honoring Jesus

I read a humorous story about a mother who was pregnant and she was having very abnormal contractions. She went to the doctor and she said "Something's going on here out of the ordinary." The doctor looked surprised when he examined her and she said, "What is it? What is it, doctor?" He said, "Well, hang on." He said, "You are pregnant with triplets, and what is happening is they're saying 'you go first, no, you go first, no, you go first'."

When God's getting ready to birth something, somebody has to go first. Somebody has to lead the pack. Somebody has to lead the way. God raises up a man or a woman or a people to lead the way and through them He will release

> *For this is he who was spoken of by the prophet Isaiah, saying: "The voice of one crying in the wilderness: 'Prepare the way of the Lord; Make His paths straight.'"*
> *Matthew 3:3*

the forerunner anointing so that they can begin to declare to the Earth what the designs and desires of Heaven are. That is the nature of the forerunner anointing. The key in leading others is to always be leading them toward Jesus. Gathering a following for oneself fails God's test for leadership and sets a person up to take a fall.

Whatever a forerunner does is done to honor the Lord. The forerunner prepares the people for the Lord. What was John's message in Matthew 3:3? Who is he preaching to? He is preaching to the people to prepare the way of the Lord and

> *Get ready. He's coming. Get things in order because when He shows up, He deserves the honor of a king. He shouldn't have to put up with a bunch of stuff. He shouldn't have to clear a lot of stuff out. Get ready. Be ready when He comes!*

to make His path straight. Now, that does not mean that the Lord is walking crooked, or that there is something wrong with the Lord. What John speaks is a call that says what is done is to be done to honor the Lord.

When the forerunner anointing is on you and operating in you, because of the revelatory insight that is given through the anointing, you are going to see before other people see. You are going to see around the curve, so to speak, you will have foresight. You will have a sense of what God wants to do before other people have the sense of what God is going to do. You must realize your foresight is to be used to honor the Lord. Since you are 'out front', if you are not careful, you can start looking back and say "Hey, folks. What are you doing back there? Can't you see what God wants to do? What is the matter with you?" You can become full of pride because you are carrying an anointing that enables you to see what they cannot see because they don't have the revelation. Pride can result in shutting down the anointing and revelation in your life.

The anointing was so strong on John the Baptist that the people started thinking, "Well, could *this* be Him? Is this Him?" I believe they were asking those questions! "Could this man, this voice, be the one who is to come? Is this the Messiah?" I think John realized that in his spirit. If you read what he shared with them, you'll see he says "No! He who comes after me is mightier than I. I am not even worthy to unlatch his shoes." John was a forerunner going before the Lord, to represent Him and to prepare His way, but he also had the realization that the Lord was always the one going before *him*.

> *Jesus said to them, "Most assuredly, I say to you, before Abraham was, I AM."*
> *John 8: 58*

Jesus said, "Before Abraham was, I am." He always existed. Listen dear Reader, the Lord was here long before any of us! He is the one who you must keep before you if you are going to go before the people and carry a forerunner anointing to lead them into the next visitation of God. It has to be done to honor the Lord. It is not about you. It is not about me. It is about Him.

> *...looking unto Jesus, the author and finisher of our faith,...*
> *Hebrews 12:2*

The New Testament is very clear about looking unto Jesus, the author and finisher of our faith. The word "author" speaks of a pioneer, one who cuts a path in a thick place so the others can follow. Jesus is the ultimate Forerunner. He is our Forerunner who went before us. So, John was the forerunner to announce the One who was the ultimate Forerunner. We always have to keep Jesus before us. It is all about Jesus, and where Jesus is lifted up honored is where the Holy Spirit is going to be working.

Honoring the Lord will save us from the issues that come from pride. John always pointed his followers to Jesus. John fathered his own disciples, and one of the forerunner characteristics is the fathering spirit. John mentored his disciples, and they followed him. But when Jesus came by one day, to paraphrase it, John said "Guys, there's the Lamb of God who takes away the sins of the world. Follow him." The forerunner recognizes his own place. The Lord must always be the one lifted up, and what we do is always to honor the Lord.

We must be like the eunuchs in the Book of Esther. If you study that story in Esther, you see a beautiful picture of a bride being prepared for the king. The role and ministry of the eunuchs was that they prepared Esther to go before the king. As they rubbed oil into her body, they realized it was the oil and not their hands that made Esther beautiful. As Eunuchs they were dead to their own desire. Their responsibility was to make the bride beautiful for their King. They were allowed to touch the "Bride to be" but with no desire for her for themselves. They were to cause her to fall in love with a man whom she had never met. That was the role of the eunuchs in the Book of Esther and that is the role of the forerunner – to prepare people to fall in love with the One they have never seen. We are to be dead to our own desires and make sure that the bride, the church, falls in love with Jesus and not with us.

So John was always careful to say, "He is mightier than I am! He must increase! I must decrease! I can't even

He must increase, but I must decrease. He who comes from above is above all; he who is of the earth is earthly and speaks of the earth. He who comes from Heaven is above all.
John 3:30-31

And he preached, saying, "There comes One after me who is mightier than I, whose sandal strap I am not worthy to stoop down and loose."
Mark 1:7

52

loose his sandals." That is something that we always have to carry in our heart if we are going to use the forerunner anointing in the way God intended us to. It is the anointing that goes before that calls for change so that the Lord can be honored when He arrives. All that the forerunner does and says is aimed at honoring the Lord.

I want to encourage you! Whatever you do, do all for the glory of God. If you have a ministry, it is not your ministry. It is His. If you have gifts, they are only gifts; you did not earn them or buy them. They were given to you. They come from Him. If you have talent, it is because of the blessing of God.

John realized that his role was to prepare the way for the Lord. We are to prepare the people to prepare the way of the Lord. But the whole purpose in preparing the people is to prepare the people to receive and welcome the Lord when He comes. The bride is beautiful as she is coming down the aisle to give herself to the groom. She has made herself ready, as beautiful as possible, robed and ready and coming to be given to her groom. There is usually an entourage of people who surround the bride preparing her, getting her ready for presentation to her groom. They surround her like bees on a bloom making sure everything is just right, but when the music starts they evaporate and disappear. Every wedding is a picture of Christ and his relationship with His church. In Ephesians 5, we are told that when Jesus comes back, He is going to receive a bride that is without spot, wrinkle, blemish or any such thing. You see, the forerunner anointing is being released in our day, to prepare the bride, to prepare the body of Christ to be ready so that when Jesus comes the mountains will be leveled, the valleys will be filled and straightened out, and everything will be smooth and polished, clean and shiny, and ready.

> *...Christ also loved the church and gave Himself for her, that He might sanctify and cleanse her with the washing of water by the word, that He might present her to Himself a glorious church, not having spot or wrinkle or any such thing, but that she should be holy and without blemish.*
> Ephesians 5: 25-27

The forerunner's mind is always set on Jesus. If we don't keep our eyes on the Lord, don't keep him first and foremost, and don't honor Him, then we'll loose what could have been. The anointing will become diminished. We've got to be laser focused in these days, and what we do must be done for Him and Him alone. The only name should be **J E S U S**. The Bible is clear that He is head of the church. The Bible is clear that He is to have the preeminence. The Bible is clear that everything in this galaxy and the universe is held together by the power of His word. The Bible is clear that all things will be summed up together as one in Him. The Bible tells us we are complete in Him. The Bible tells us that we've been given all things that pertain to life and godliness through the knowledge of Him. It is all about Him. The forerunner anointing recognizes that. We must be like John the Baptist. The Lord must increase, and we must decrease.

It's a good thing when people start looking at a Christian and start seeing Jesus. They looked at John the Baptist and thought he could be the Messiah because there was so much God on his life. *We* want that. *We* want to reflect the image of Christ in this earth. *We* are complete in Him. *We* want to be so close to the Lord that we reflect His glory in the Earth. What you *don't* want is to start thinking you are as powerful as He is. That's where you fall down, and that's where the downfall comes. The moment it stops being about Jesus and starts being about someone that God is using, then that person might get lifted up but the anointing starts declining. Only as you continue to lift Jesus up will Jesus continue to lift you up. There is always a danger at casting your gaze upon someone the Lord is using. First, it causes you to become wrongly focused. Secondly, if they fall, you may tumble with them due to the disillusionment that such a case unleashes on people who are wrongly focused. We honor those God uses, but always with a lesser honor than our heart holds for Jesus.

The people in the book of Acts took note of those ignorant unlearned men that smelled of fish, the disciples, and knew they had been with Jesus. That's different than calling the men "Jesus". The Lord wants to so purify His bride, the church, that all of a sudden the world will start looking at the church and saying 'Jesus!' If in their ignorance they attempt to ascribe to us what only belongs to Him, we will be quick to bow at His feet and encourage them to join us. That's the forerunner. We prepare the people to be prepared for him. We want them to see Jesus in us, so that they say 'Wow! They look like Jesus!'. But we will quickly attest that we are just a reflector of the Lord's glory. The forerunner understands this principle and always honors the Lord.

A Personal Prayer

Father God, I ask in the name of Jesus that you would bless me and that your fire would burn in my heart. Lord, I pray that I would carry a torch for you – that I would be a light in a dark place. Father, I pray I would be carried by the wind of your Spirit to the places you want to send me and used the way you want to use me. Lord, I pray that I would live in such a way that your glory would be manifest in my life. Lord, I do not want to grab for your glory, but Lord, I do want to be where your glory is poured out. Lord, I do not want to touch your glory, but I want your glory to touch me. I just ask that you would raise me up and make me a forerunner, Lord, to be prepared and to prepare people to prepare for your arrival – for you're soon coming! Lord, I pray for increased revelation and for angelic visitation. I pray for the outpouring of your Spirit in my life. I pray for the operation of spiritual gifts in my life. I pray for the signs and wonders and miracles to flow in my life. I desire that the Lord Jesus always have the highest honor in my heart. I pray that he would never be found sharing my heart's affection with the love that is to be solely his. May I decreas, and may He increase in my life. I thank you, Lord Jesus, and I bless your name.

Chapter Seven

The Prophetic

> But what did you go out to see? A prophet? Yes, I say to you, and more than a prophet.
> Matthew 11:9

John the Baptist's message was strongly prophetic; *He is coming!* In Matthew 11:9, Jesus himself referred to John as a prophet. John prophetically declared things that would take place in the future. He did it with passion, without compromise, and with integrity and accuracy. He announced the desire of the Lord over the people preaching, "He's going to baptize you with the Holy Spirit and fire." He was announcing something God was about to do. The forerunner anointing carries with it the prophetic element. When someone speaks what God has spoken to them that a certain event is about to happen and then the event happens, that's prophetic. The creation of the universe came about as a result of God speaking, and then what He spoke happened. That's the operation of the prophetic. And so forerunner anointing releases the prophetic message, "Prepare the way of the Lord, He's coming!" John also carried the message, "Flee from the wrath to come." That's prophetic. Judgment is coming. He is coming. He's not here yet, but when He comes *He will* baptize you with the Holy Ghost and with fire. *He will* gather his wheat in his barn, *He will* burn the chaff with unquenchable fire. These *He wills* are prophetic in their nature. The message is prophetic.

> He will also go before Him in the spirit and power of Elijah, ... to make ready a people prepared for the Lord."
> Luke 1:17
>
> Jesus answered and said to them, "Indeed, Elijah is coming first and will restore all things.
> Matthew 17:11

Now it's interesting that Jesus said Elijah must first come to restore all things. Elijah was a major prophetic figure in the Old Testament, and Moses was the major Law figure. When you think of the Office of Prophet in the Old Testament, Elijah is foremost. When you think about Law, Moses is the foremost. At the transfiguration, who was represented with Jesus? Moses represents the law, the written word of God. Elijah represents the prophets, the spoken word of God. Jesus represents the living word of God, the eternal logos. The three are together at the transfiguration. We are told, in Luke 1:17, that before the first coming of Jesus the spirit of Elijah rested on John the Baptist. Elijah was prophetic. John's message was prophetic.

John was the forerunner before the first coming of Jesus, and Jesus said that Elijah must first come and restore all things. Heaven will receive Jesus until the restoration of all things. Therefore, before the return of Jesus, the second coming of Jesus, there will also be an outpouring of the Spirit of Elijah on the church to a body of forerunners to prepare the earth for the coming of the King.

There have always been glimpses of prophecy in operation in the modern church, but in a smaller measure than what we are seeing now. In the 1900s, especially in the middle of the century, through the healing evangelists and the healing revival, many of the prophetic gifts began to be restored to the church in a measure not seen since the early church. Then, in the this generation, all of a sudden out of nowhere, the prophetic gifts really starting coming into view as being for the whole body. God has released an anointing to shake the church up and to awaken her and to say,"You are a prophetic people," and to restore the prophetic gifts. And so, there's been a lot more teaching and preaching about the gift of prophecy, the office of the prophetic, and the prophetic among God's people. And yes! God still ministers through prophetic ministry. It is a very valid part of the Scripture and is to be a very vibrant part of New Testament Christianity. What we've seen in the last 25 years or so is literally the restoration of the prophetic ministry in the church as part of the five-fold ministry: the apostle, the prophet, the evangelist, the pastor, and the teacher.

The church through the centuries had distanced herself from the full five fold ministry office gifts, but our more recent history records God redeeming and

> Hearing the Word in Latin was like hearing the message in tongues every Sunday without an interpreter!

restoring them and bringing them cohesively back together and

57

functioning in the body. The teaching gift was restored when the Bible was translated into the language of the people. Before that is was just in Latin; the people had to hear it in Latin which meant nothing to them! God moved supernaturally to give wisdom to men and Johannes Gutenberg invented the printing press and printed the Bible in the language of the people. Suddenly, they could be taught!

Historically, in the days before the Protestant reformation, the church believed no one could get to God except through the priests. The Protestant Reformation started by Martin Luther, restored ministry to the people, the lay ministry to the people, the shepherding gift. God raised up people like Charles Finney, the Wesleys, D.L. Moody, and others that carried the anointing of an evangelist and reminded the church that we are to be casting the net to catch sinners who are outside the four walls of the building that had become seen as the church. The church wasn't to be so secluded and separate that the lost couldn't come.

So there was the restoration of the teaching, of the pastoral, the evangelistic, and then in the past century, the restoration of the charismatic gifts to a greater degree that opened the door for the prophetic. In the last 10 or 15 years, do you know what everything has been about? The apostolic! If we are now in the

> *And He Himself gave some to be apostles, some prophets, some evangelists, and some pastors and teachers, for the equipping of the saints for the work of ministry, for the edifying of the body of Christ, till we all come to the unity of the faith and of the knowledge of the Son of God, to a perfect man, to the measure of the stature of the fullness of Christ; but, speaking the truth in love, may grow up in all things into Him who is the head— Christ— from whom the whole body, joined and knit together by what every joint supplies, according to the effective working by which every part does its share, causes growth of the body for the edifying of itself in love.*
> *Ephesians 4: 11-14, 16*

age of the apostolic reformation and restoration, that tells us something! In Ephesians 4, we are told that He gave gifts to us, until we *all* come together in the unity of faith to be a true reflection of Christ in the earth. I know this is a simplified view of restoration and is not intended to say that there were not people throughout the age of the church who did

58

not function as apostles, prophets, evangelists, pastors, and teachers. The restoration of all things has to do with completeness and fullness. It is about all of it beginning to work together and to have the place in the body that God intends. There are scholars skilled in history who can bring out so many wonderful people (forerunners), places, and events that God has used to bring about change. I am not saying that there were times when these office gifts did not exist; I am saying that there were times that the church did not recognize, receive, or relate to them. I believe that there has always been and always will be a remnant who are carrying the truth of God. For the most part, these remnant people have been and today are forerunners in the area of revelation that they are carrying.

Remember, Chapter Four of Ephesians tells us that when the church has been made pure, love will be operating within her, and she will be equipped by full five-fold ministry. As a result, she will be able to stand up and be the reflection of Christ in the Earth without any spot, blemish, or any such thing. Then it will be time to sound the trumpet and have a wedding! It is important to understand the day in which we are living.

'Blessed are those who are called to the marriage supper of the Lamb!' " And he said to me, "These are the true sayings of God." And I fell at his feet to worship him. But he said to me, "See that you do not do that! I am your fellow servant, and of your brethren who have the testimony of Jesus. Worship God! For the testimony of Jesus is the spirit of prophecy."
Revelation 19:9-10

The forerunner anointing is strongly prophetic. Revelation 19:10 tells us the testimony of Jesus is the spirit of prophecy. The true prophetic will always come back and point to Jesus. Everything is going to be summed up in Him, and then the kingdom will be delivered to the Father. The prophetic declares what God wants, His plans and his purposes. So, God begins releasing the forerunner anointing on His people, and they began to stand up declaring, proclaiming, and decreeing what God wants and what God is about to do. They declare the next shift, the next adjustment and alignment that is required for the church to become who God wants her to become.

A Personal Prayer

Dear Lord, I want to hear your voice. I want to speak what you tell me to speak. I thank you that I am a prophetic person. I was made to experience communication with you. May your revelation flow into my spirit and be spoken out my mouth in your time and in your way. I desire that the spirit of revelation, wisdom, and knowledge be given to me to understand your plans and purposes during this season of my life. Thank you that you are working through your church to restore the flow of the prophetic so that your "now" voice can be heard. Please remove any barriers that would blind me from seeing what you are doing or hearing what you are saying. I ask this in Jesus' name, amen!

Chapter Eight

Unorthodox—Welcoming the "Wild" and Weird

Has anyone ever told you that you were weird for what you believed? Have they accused you of being on the wild side when it comes to your worship of Jesus? Be encouraged, you are not the first to be seen in such a way. Now, if the

Now John himself was clothed in camel's hair, with a leather belt around his waist; and his food was locusts and wild honey. Matthew 3:4

people that are called wild and weird are telling you that you are too far out there, it may be that you need to reel in a few feet of line. But let's face it, many of our brothers and sisters consider us a little crazy for doing what we do the way we do it. The forerunner anointing is often bestowed upon obscure people from obscure places who are often misunderstood. We have already talked about that earlier in this book. But forerunners are not only often the obscure but also the outrageous! You have to admit that a little old lady and little old man having a baby after they start drawing social security is a little out there. Such was the case for Zacharias and Elizabeth. A daddy not being allowed to speak until his son is born is a little weird. A teenage girl who is pregnant without ever having a sexual relationship could easily be classified as wild imagination. Yet, these are some of the circumstances that surrounded the births of John and Jesus. The forerunner anointing is unorthodox, different, radical, and non-mainstream. It is not going to look like what you are used to seeing. It is not going to feel like what you are used to feeling. It is going to be different. John, himself, was clothed in camel's hair with a leather belt around his waste, and his food

John was just *not* your regular run of the mill, cut from the cloth, kind of preacher guy. He was not necessarily polished, suave and debonair – he was *different*.

was locusts and wild honey. His clothes and diet reflected where he came from. He dressed like a wild man because he was from the wilderness. John was *a little bit different*. Some might say he was quite eccentric. He was different, unorthodox, and radical. His pulpit was out in the wilderness. His diet was grasshoppers and wild honey. He knew what it was like to have to fight bees to get to honey. He wore camel's hair, rough coarse camel's hair!

Why Do They Wear What They Wear?

We need to understand that the forerunner will be different. The forerunner is the person who goes beforehand to say, "Hey! Something is about to change! Things are going to be different!" The forerunner will be different because they will reflect the message they carry. When you are really carrying a forerunner anointing and the forerunner message, the message just begins to impact everything about you. I have noticed that what people are carrying in the spirit sometimes breaks out in the natural by the way they dress. What they sense inside of them is so radically different that sometimes it just breaks out through their clothes. Typically, this changes as they work through their call and identity. It is wrong to see this as rebellion. In some cases, it can be a rebellious statement, but among the Lord's emerging warriors there are many young people who are expressing their radical passion in unorthodox ways. Do some go too far? Sure, they do. But we must not make the mistake of so focusing on the outward man that we are blind to what the Spirit of God is doing inside the hearts of this arising generation. I would also add a word of admonition to you younger warriors as well. Don't make the mistake of failing to respect what the older generation has carried and still carries. I am not talking about forfeiting all your liberty but forging ahead in love desiring to bring the generations together.

Bury Your Girdle

Understanding the unorthodox and radical part of forerunning will help you understand some of the things Jeremiah did such as going down to the river and burying his girdle and then going back and digging it up. God told him to do some pretty radical stuff, which may be the reason the next book he wrote was about crying, the book of Lamentations. John the Baptizer was an unusual person. He was different. He was unorthodox. He was radical. He was non-mainstream. Religion hated John, so much that they finally cut off his head.

Sometimes when God wants to birth something to bring about a lot of change, He uses a sledgehammer. He knows what it is going to take to get us out of our comfort zones, so we are willing to change. In John's time there were the religious leaders, walking down the street with their long flowing gowns and phylacteries. They were very religious. Even the word "phylacteries" sounds stuck-up, doesn't it? They even had people who would go before them announcing their arrival. They had their own forerunners, who would proclaim "Clear the street; clear the street. The Pharisees are coming; the Sadducees are on the way. Clear the street; clear the street; clear the street."

When God decided He wanted to come down to Earth, He sent a forerunner and gave him a camel-hair coat. He gave him fried grasshoppers, probably upsized! He put him out in the wilderness. He said, "I am going to send my son, and he is going to be born surrounded by animals and manure." That is a little radical. That is a little different. That is a little unorthodox. But, it was God. Sometimes when we struggle with whom God uses we tend to be critical, and we are tempted to become judgmental. We complain that what we see is just radical, unorthodox, not mainstream, and just 'out there'. But, sometimes it is God! I think that God rather enjoys tearing up the boxes we try to build to contain who He is and what He does.

The Deathblow to Dignity

God knows how to deal the deathblow to our dignity. Back in 1997 when I was in a season of desperation, God began showing me that a lot of what I was doing in the ministry was for the pat on the back, for my own ego. I needed to feel good about myself. I needed to hear that I was doing a good job. I was getting a lot of my security from the sheep instead of the Shepherd.

God began dealing with me, and I became broken, realizing that I was using what the Lord had given me for my own inner satisfaction instead of desiring to please Him. I finally got to the point that I thought, "Lord if there is not more than this, I am ready to quit. I just cannot go on anymore. I am tired of this ministerial bag of tricks. I cannot play in the system anymore. No more church games, God. If what I read in the Book of Acts is for today, I want it!" Well, the Lord knows how to break down our pride and bring us to the point that we are ready to receive what He wants to give us.

That is the reason that one Monday morning a little guy came into my office. His clothes looked like they had not been washed in a month. He had grease and dirt caked up under his fingernails. He needed a haircut, shampoo and a shave. He needed a few trips to the dentist. He came into my office with cigarettes in his shirt pocket.

He came into my office for me to pray for him. While we were sitting there, I heard the Lord say, "Have *him* pray for *you*." Well, for me to hear the Lord's voice at that time – that was a startling thing. But I knew it was God. I struggled but it was clear, "Have *him* pray for *you*."

Finally, after squirming awhile, I said, "Sir, I think the Lord wants you to pray for *me*!" He asked, "You want *me* to pray for *you*?" He was very intimidated because he sat in my office surrounded by thousands of books, some of them really thick books! I had my diplomas hung up on the wall with my doctorate degree hanging high and lifted up. I sat prim and proper in my nice suit in my inner-office, which was part of my bigger office. I had standing in the community, name recognition, and a country club membership. He was very intimidated. He had come for prayer from me and now the tables had turned, and it was God who did the turning.

After a few moments, he stood and walked over to where I was sitting. He dropped to his knees and bowed his head. With his hands and greasy fingernails, he took my hands into his. He began praying, "Father, Dear God, baptize this man with the Holy Ghost. Help him to speak in tongues. Give him an anointing to cast out devils. Let there be an anointing on his life to heal the sick." He prayed like that. He got through and I said, "Well... I appreciate that, brother." But, his prayer was like a sledgehammer that caused the walls to start to crack. I did not understand it right then, but God needed somebody who had guts enough to pray for me what needed praying. That little man was sent by God into my life to release that prayer over me. It turned out to be a wonderfully, humbling experience. We often miss some great gifts by thinking that the wrapping on the box indicates that there can't be much inside.

The forerunner anointing gives its carrier the unction to do what God wants done, and sometimes it is unorthodox. It is not mainstream. It does not look normal. God knows what it is going to take to get you out of your comfort zone, to resurrect you out of your rut, and break you up on the inside, so He can put you together the way He wants to put you together. He deals the deathblow to dignity and sophistication and religion. Then, what He does is take all your preparation, training, and experience, and He baptizes it so He can use it in the way that He meant for it to be used in the beginning. This is restoration, and God will even use people with issues to bring it about in your life. As a matter of fact, the only people He has to use are people with issues! Some of us have just acquired the ability to paint our issues with a prettier coat of paint or put prettier wrapping paper on them.

Speak Plainly Please!

We need to realize that God knows what it takes to penetrate the lost world around us. Sometimes, we get so caught up with 'churchianity' that we forget why the church is here. It is here for all those lost people out there that do not know about the Lord, and do not know that Jesus died for them. There was an evangelist who went up into the rural mountains. He was a city slicker, and he just knew he was going to evangelize those mountain folks. He walked way back in the mountains. He came up to a little cabin, and there was a man in overalls sitting on the front porch whittling on a stick of wood. The evangelist said, "Sir, are you lost?" The whittler said, "No. I ain't lost. I have been here all my life. I know right where I am." "Well, that is not what I mean. I mean are you a Christian?" said the evangelist. The whittler said, "No! Old Ned Christian, he lives three ridges over, over there ,you might want to visit with him." "No, no! That is not what I mean. I mean are you ready for the judgment day?" said the exasperated evangelist. The whittler asked, "Well, when is it?" The evangelist excitedly said, "Well, it could be today, or it could be tomorrow!" Calmly, the whittler replied, "Well, I tell you what...you let me know when, and I will tell my wife. She'll probably want to go both days."

Sometimes our church language is so confusing to the lost that we can't even communicate with them. The Pharisees and Sadducees were parading up and down the streets of Jerusalem in their religious piety, and the people were out there hungering, craving and wanting to know God. Jesus said the religious leaders of his day stood in the door and would not let him in. So God sent somebody out in the wilderness who wore a camel's hair jacket, put on a leather belt, got some wild grasshoppers for a meal , so the people could relate to him. This man had something to say that they wanted to hear. John the Baptist carried the forerunner anointing that would lead them where their hearts cried to go. He was plain spoken, and the people understood what he had to say.

It does not matter who you are. It does not matter where you have been. It does not matter what you have become. God can use you if you will just humble yourself. He is preparing people to be preparers of the people. He is releasing the spirit of Elijah, the forerunner anointing, and it is for us.

Dare to be Different

All through the Bible, God called people to do things that had never been done before. He told Noah, "I want you to build an Ark. Build it over here on dry ground. There is going to be a flood." It had never even rained on Earth!

God told Abraham, "Just start traveling; I will tell you later on where you are going. Just get going." That was a little different for Abraham! God told Moses, "Throw down that rod and it will turn into a snake." What happened was so strange that Moses fled! Later God told Moses, "Hold up that rod, and I will part the Red Sea." God told Joshua, "You and all the soldiers, march around the city seven times, do not say a word, and the walls will fall." Now, *that* was a little on the weird side. Elisha told Naaman, "Go and wash in the Jordan seven times, and your flesh shall be restored to you, and you shall be clean." Washing in a dirty river to cure leprosy? The thought was so strange to Naaman that at first he refused to do it.

John the Baptist shows up spruced up in camel hair saying, "Get ready, God is coming." The anointing was so powerful on him that the people were compelled to believe him! Jesus shows up, spits in the eye of a blind man, and he is healed! This method of healing ministry is still not popularly used. This was just one of many unorthodox practices and teachings. The people said, "We have never seen things like this. Strange things have happened in our midst this day!" Then, they followed Jesus!

> It was God for Noah.
> It was God for Moses.
> It was God for Joshua.
> It was God for Elijah.
> It was God for Elisha.
> It was God for John.
> It was God for Jesus.
> It was God for the early church.
> It is God today!

If you study the Day of Pentecost, you'll discover that it was not just your average Joe kind of day either: the sound of a wind filling a room, cloven tongues of fire, people speaking languages they never learned, strange babble, strange talk! What did the world say? The world said, "These people must be drunk." But guess what it was? It was God. It was God the whole time. Others who sensed their spirits stirred, got on board for the ride of their lives. Sometimes, it is unorthodox; sometimes, it is different; sometimes, it is non-mainstream; and sometimes, it is radical; yet it is God.

A Personal Prayer

Lord, I want it; I want it, Lord! You must increase. I must decrease. Lord, if you need to deal with dignity, if you need to deal with the stuff, the junk that stands in my way of being a prepared person then do it! Just remove the mountains of pride. Fill in the valleys of self-pity. Straighten out the crookedness of unrighteousness, Lord. Sand away on those areas Lord, which are still roughshod. Prepare me, Lord, so that I can prepare for what you want to do in your next visitation. Oh Lord, change me. Change me; make me more like yourself.

Father God, right now, I just welcome the ministry of your Holy Spirit! I thank you that you will soothe, comfort and encourage me right now. I thank you, Lord, that your sufficiency and your grace is filling my heart and life right now, and that you are showing how great you are through your grace. Lord, I pray that you would bless me so that I can be a blessing to others. I thank you Lord Jesus Christ, and I bless your name!

Chapter Nine

Exposing Religion and Position Consciousness

Another characteristic of the forerunner anointing is that it exposes religion and position consciousness. Matthew 3:7 tells us John's reaction to seeing the Pharisees and Sadducees. Did John try to butter them up so he could get more offering from them? No! He called them a bunch of snakes! Now, I'm not suggesting that you do this at your next meeting. John was anointed to say what he said. He was not a reed shaking in the wind. He was bold and courageous.

> *But when he saw many of the Pharisees and Sadducees coming to his baptism, he said to them, "Brood of vipers! Who warned you to flee from the wrath to come?"*
> *Matthew 3:7*
>
> *"Therefore bear fruits worthy of repentance, and do not think to say to yourselves, 'We have Abraham as our father.' For I say to you that God is able to raise up children to Abraham from these stones."*
> *Matthew 3:8-9*

If the Pharisees were fishing for compliments, they went home with their stringers empty after visiting with John. John confronted their position consciousness by letting them know that their claim to God's favor as children of Abraham was no longer valid. John was not afraid to confront religion. By religion, I am referring to dead works done to appease or please God, or rituals and traditions that interfere with the reception of truth. Religion also involves practices that are done to please or impress man while ignoring God. John was not afraid to level the playing field and say to the Pharisees and Sadducees, "Your position will not get you into Heaven. The titles that you are dragging around will not get you anywhere in the Kingdom." Their robes that sparkled of status and pomp did not move John in the least. Silk or camel's hair was not and is still not the issue. Steak or grasshoppers was not and is still not the issue. The wilderness or the city streets was not and is still not the issue. Education or heritage was not and is still not the issue. The issue was and still is about the heart, for out of it flow the issues of life.

69

Self Exaltation

Being filled with religion and position consciousness will make us want to lift ourselves up. When the forerunner anointing is released on us, our hearts realize that He must increase and we must decrease. Who is one that is supposed to lift us up? The Bible says, "Humble yourself under the mighty hand of God, and He will exalt you in due time." When God exalts you, there is not a thing in the world a man can do about it. But, if a man exalts you, all that has to happen is for the hand of man to move and you are gone! When the hand of God raises you up, no man can pull you down.

The Pharisees and Sadducees were two different religious groups. The Pharisees were very strict law keepers. As I have heard Jack Taylor say, "They were fair, you see?" The Sadducees did not believe in the Resurrection. "They were sad, you see?" The Pharisees and the Sadducees had different doctrinal beliefs, they dressed differently, and they disagreed with one another. Paul used this to his advantage on one occasion to get the Pharisees and Sadducees arguing with each other so they would draw the attention off him. They were debaters, they were religious, and Jesus did not say anything good about the Pharisees and Sadducees because He recognized the influence of religion over their lives.

> 'Religion' means you think you always have to do more – you are never satisfied because you think God is never satisfied!

Religion can strip you of the power of hope and make you so works driven that you feel like there is no way you can ever do enough to please God. You feel like you have to do something more for God to accept you. You have to be just a little bit better. Religion refuses to see the Lord as a loving, Heavenly Father, who dispenses His grace and mercy to His children to enable them to serve Him out of love, not out of intimidation and fear. As it has been said by so many, religion is spelled D-O, but true Christianity is spelled D-O-N-E. It is not about what we do for Him, it is about what He has done for us. When we rest in what He has done for us, then we experience the

70

freedom to do what we were created to do for Him. Really, He does the work through us!

Long Accusing Fingers

The Pharisees and Sadducees pointed long, accusing fingers at people and had a long list of regulations that, because of their position in the synagogue, only they could keep. And even then they invented loopholes for themselves to justify their own failures. They conveniently adjusted their beliefs to accommodate their inadequacies while holding others to the full measure of their regulations. That is what religion does. It makes you think it is *others'* sin that is always ugly, and yours is not so bad because "I understand why I do what I do". Religion causes us to fabricate rules and regulations that cannot be found in the Scripture creating burdens for others and ourselves. Jesus exposed the Pharisees and Sadducees for doing this.

Jesus said this system of belief will send you across the ocean to change somebody to be like you, and then you will stand in the way of those who really want to know God. Jesus, however, will send you across the ocean to change people to be like Him. The Gospel is for everyone. Religion tends to concentrate on people who can reproduce the system. When religion showed up at John's doorstep he recognized it. John's thoughts must have been "You are *not* going to intimidate me. You are *not* going to make me think that I am not doing what God is telling me to do. You are *not* going to shut down this ministry. If you are going to be a part of this, you *have* to change." That was John's message. His fearlessness toward men was rooted in his reverential fear of God.

John was not going to forfeit his destiny to people who had no intention of finding theirs. Both, Jesus and John, knew what they had been called to do and were committed to seeing that call fulfilled obediently. Jesus was so loving and merciful and kind and gracious. That is, until He stood in the face of religion! He never backed down to religion. Religion was the one thing that Satan was using to keep people from coming to Jesus. Jesus' tolerance level for religion was extremely low. In Matthew 15, Jesus denounced the Pharisees for their traditions.

71

There is nothing wrong with a tradition, but when it is exalted over truth, that tradition becomes an idol in your life, and you become a breaker of the second commandment.[Q] Remember, when the forerunner anointing is released God prepares the preparer first. Before we go around pointing a finger at the religion that we do not like, we have to allow Him to put His finger on the religion in our

> *Hypocrites! Well did Isaiah prophesy about you, saying: 'These people draw near to Me with their mouth, And honor Me with their lips, But their heart is far from Me. And in vain they worship Me, Teaching as doctrines the commandments of men.'*
> Matthew 15:7-9

own hearts. The forerunner anointing uncompromisingly exposes religion and position consciousness. Before we deal with it in others, however, we must first deal with it in ourselves.

Doomed to Condemnation

Religion causes you to focus on failures, like little Tommy who came up to the preacher after the service and said, "When I get big, I am going to give you a lot of money." The preacher said, "Well that is very kind of you; why would you do that?" Tommy said, "Because my daddy said you are the poorest preacher he has ever heard." Can you imagine how that preacher must have felt? That is the way religion makes you feel, inadequate, not able to measure up before God, a failure. Of course, this is one of the purposes of the law of God. It exposes our sin and shows us where we have fallen short. But we cannot stop with the law, or we are doomed to live under condemnation. We began with the law but move to grace through repentance. That was John's message – repent. Religion stops with the law and doesn't move on to grace. The other extreme is standing in grace without ever being confronted by the law. This leads to unholy living. The law knocks us down, and grace picks us up!

[Q] *What traditions in your own life hinder your acceptance of other Christians and their traditions? How do you think the Lord would like you to deal with those traditions?*

A religious spirit can cause you to look at what you are doing and compare others to you instead of looking at Jesus and comparing yourself to him. Erroneous thinking makes us think "You are not like me, because if you were really in on what God is doing, you would be where I am. You would be doing what I am doing."

I thank God for my heritage, but I have realized that the Kingdom is not about heritage. It is about Jesus. It is about unity within the body of Christ and tearing down the walls that divide us. It does not mean that everyone is going to believe just the same or look just the same. That is what religion wants us to do, to all look and act the same. Religion wants to make external our characteristics the measures of how spiritual we are and measures of whether or not God will accept us at all. It is not about uniformity but unity that the Spirit is bringing about in our day. This is what Jesus prayed for in John 17. It is where Paul said the church was headed in Ephesians 4.

Stop Attacking the Bride

Then Saul, still breathing threats and murder against the disciples of the Lord, ... came near Damascus, and suddenly a light shone around him from Heaven. Then he fell to the ground, and heard a voice saying to him, "Saul, Saul, why are you persecuting Me?" Acts 9:1,3-4

One day in the spring of 1997, the Lord spoke to me that I had no business attacking his bride. I was stunned. I knew how I would feel if someone started attacking and saying bad things about my wife. This is when I realized that I had been working *against* the One I claimed to be working *for*. Jesus takes it personally when we persecute His bride. Paul was persecuting the church yet Jesus asked him, "Why are you persecuting me?" He takes it personally when we attack his bride. At times, I would use the pulpit to cause the congregation to harbor wrong feelings toward the church down the road because there were certain doctrinal areas where I was sure they were in error. Of course, I had to protect my flock, right? No! I was wrong in what I did and why I did it. I started repenting. God dealt with me about denominational pride. On a Sunday morning at the

73

conclusion of the service, I shared with my congregation that I had been wrong. I asked them to forgive me for all the times that I had caused them, through my preaching to harbor ill feelings toward others in the body of Christ. I shared with them what the Lord had told me.

The following Saturday morning, I attended the local Promise Keepers meeting. I stood in that restaurant and asked all those present to forgive me for the times I had spoken against them because they differed from me in certain doctrinal beliefs. The next morning on my weekly Sunday morning radio broadcast, I repeated my repentance over the airwaves to the entire listening area. It was a time when the fallow ground was being plowed up in my heart. It hurt, but it hurt good! I repented so much, I started being proud about being good at repenting. Then, the Lord had to deal with me about being proud about my repentance! This just goes to show that we must live on our faces before God. Moment by moment, we must try to live in the consciousness of God and to be more like Jesus. When we take our eyes off Him and place them on anything or anyone else, we become vulnerable to the trappings of a religious spirit.

Not long after the Lord started tearing down these walls in my heart, I was in a hospital room visiting with a lady who was a member of the Baptist church I was pastoring at the time. A Church of God preacher came into the room. He was the volunteer chaplain for that week. He was a man that I had been praying with weekly, along with several other pastors, for several months. I loved my brother. He came in as the volunteer chaplain and said, "Before I go, I would like to have a word of prayer with you." So he led us in prayer.

Now, this lady was a sweet lady who had never missed a church service. She was a faithful giver, was faithful to the church, loved the church and the people of her church. But, when the Church of God pastor walked out the door, and the door had barely closed behind him, she said, "I bet his prayer didn't even make it to the ceiling." My heart dropped, for several reasons. First of all, I heard in her what I knew had been so much in me. Second of all, that was *my brother*, and I knew he was a man of God!

I shared with her that I knew this brother, that he loved the Lord, and that we were very blessed he would pray with us. However, I had to be careful not to judge her because I was not many days removed from where she was. I believe all of us carry traces of thinking that we are better than others. We may think, "Well, if they really had revelation, we know where *they* would be going to church." Oh really? Is it not interesting that we can know what somebody's God-given destiny is? God forgive us for our presumption and judgment.

I heard the fabled story of the man who retired. He decided that he was tired of shaving and was going to go to the barber shop and pay somebody to give him a shave. So he went down to a barber shop owned by a Baptist preacher and his wife named Grace. It just so happened that Grace gave him a shave that morning. When she got through, she charged him $20. He thought that was extremely expensive, but he reluctantly paid her. When he awakened the next morning, he rubbed his face and there was not a whisker to be found. He thought, "Wow, what a shave!" The next day he awakened and his face was still smoothly shaven with not a whisker to be found.

Finally, after two weeks, with his face still so smooth and not a whisker to be found, he said, "I thought $20 was a lot, but I am feeling like I am getting my money's worth!" So he dropped by the barber shop and he said, "I have to ask you this – it has been two weeks and my face is still smooth. How did you do that?" She said, "Oh sir, do you not understand? You were shaved by Grace, and once shaved always shaved." You know, with *my* Baptist foundation I really like that story. We all feel strongly about our beliefs, as we should. But we must not break fellowship with our brother over something that is not the basis of relationship with our God.

> Whoever believes that Jesus is the Christ is born of God, and everyone who loves Him who begot also loves him who is begotten of Him. By this we know that we love the children of God,
> 1 John 5:1-2

If we are not careful, we separate ourselves from other people based on the minors we believe, when the only important thing is what we believe about Jesus. The aged Apostle John wrote that

75

those who believe in Jesus love the children of God. The forerunner anointing makes you aware that you might be right in what you believe, but you are not right in the way you are carrying what you believe. God never gave us his doctrine to use as swords against our brothers and sisters. If you are doing that, you are wielding the sword in the wrong direction. You belong to Him. If you belong to Him and I belong to Him, then you and I are brothers and sisters. We are in the same family and we are going to spend eternity together. It might be a good idea if we could learn to get along a little bit better here on Earth.

Family Heritage

We might be surprised at how much pain we avoid and how much blessing we receive because of our relatives' walk with God. Sometimes we are mistaken and think we are blessed because of who we are, and do not realize that it might be because of Grandma's walk and her prayers that are covering us.[Q] Thank God for a godly family heritage, but then again, do not think for a moment because of Grandma's getting into Heaven that you are going to get in. You may have had a better opportunity because you have heard the Gospel, and it is ingrained in your family heritage, but unless you trust Jesus as your Lord and Savior, you will not get into Heaven.

However, do not make the mistake of thinking that where you are from is more important than where you are going. We cannot have the mentality that because mom or dad believed one way, that we must believe the same way. God has given us free will, and we must make up our own minds about our beliefs. We do not need to hang onto family heritage just to continue family traditions. The Holy Spirit will guide us!

Heaven's plans unfold from God's heart as He moves across the galaxies touching lives down here to do what is desired up there. The hand of God exalts and puts people into places just like He did John the Baptist. God reached down and told Zacharias before baby John was

---

[Q] *Who do you remember in your family heritage that you knew was a Christian? When was the last time you thanked the Lord for them?*

ever conceived that he would have a son. God reached down into Elizabeth's womb and touched that baby – that little baby in momma's womb, filled him with the Holy Ghost, and formed him with the DNA that caused him to be the one to announce and proclaim that Jesus was coming!

John the Baptist had an impressive heritage. His father served in the temple. His mother loved God. However, he knew that he as an individual was responsible to the Lord to hear the call God had on his life. He had to be willing to wear that camel's hair and to eat those grasshoppers and that wild honey, and when the time came he had to be willing to stand against the religion of the day. He had to be willing to have his head severed from his shoulders because he was a carrier of an anointing proclaiming, "Christ has come."

Achievements and Ladder Climbing

The Bible is very clear about giving honor where honor is due. The Bible is also very clear about the origin of praise for accomplishments. Sometimes we give too much importance to what we have achieved. My nine years of college and Bible seminary education was hard work and sacrifice. I walked across the platform on different occasions and got those degrees, and I had a certain amount of pride because I had worked so hard to get them. I got the diplomas, put them in nice gold frames, and hung them on the wall in my office behind my chair so that when somebody was sitting with me they would see all the evidence that showed I was prepared. I am still proud of my accomplishments in a good way. I thank God for giving me the grace and strength to be able get those degrees, and getting them has been very helpful and beneficial for me in many ways. But for a season, I belonged to them instead of them belonging to me.

In 1997, the Lord began exposing my heart and I realized that I was looking at those degrees for the fulfillment that I was supposed to be seeking from Him. I was looking to my achievements for fulfillment instead of looking to *what He had done for me*. This was not intentional but still harmful. In a way, I was focusing on what I had done for him

> *For we are the circumcision, who worship God in the Spirit, rejoice in Christ Jesus, and have no confidence in the flesh, though I also might have confidence in the flesh. If anyone else thinks he may have confidence in the flesh, I more so: circumcised the eighth day, of the stock of Israel, of the tribe of Benjamin, a Hebrew of the Hebrews; concerning the law, a Pharisee; concerning zeal, persecuting the church; concerning the righteousness which is in the law, blameless. But what things were gain to me, these I have counted loss for Christ. Yet indeed I also count all things loss for the excellence of the knowledge of Christ Jesus my Lord, for whom I have suffered the loss of all things, and count them as rubbish, that I may gain Christ and be found in Him, not having my own righteousness, which is from the law, but that which is through faith in Christ, the righteousness which is from God by faith;*
> Philippians 3:3-9

instead of what he had done for me. I did not realize that I was holding up my achievements in front of the cross. The Lord began to show me that I was striving, elbowing, climbing, and struggling to "get ahead."

When you are running in your own race, you struggle to get out in front of the rest of the people. That is not the kind of forerunner we are talking about. We are talking about the forerunner God looks upon and says, "I want to prepare you, equip you, and change you so I can trust you to serve me." Paul tells us of his own struggle with pride in the list of his accomplishments in the third chapter of Philippians.

I remember the day that I went over to that wall and removed those diplomas. It was not wrong to have them hanging on the wall, but I needed to take them down. I needed to take them down because they needed to be taken down in my heart. Before I could do that, the Lord had to break down my pride over what I had achieved, and had worked hard to accomplish. God then started to use all that preparation, study, and training in a way that would glorify Him.

Pride in Spiritual Gifts

Religion wants us to have confidence in the flesh. Religion can also cause you to have confidence in your spiritual gifts. You can get in the flesh with your spiritual gifts and become proud about the spiritual gifts you carry or the gifts, talents, and abilities that God has given you. God is a lot more concerned about our character than he is our giftedness. He is a lot more concerned about our becoming more like Christ than he is about what we are able to accomplish or achieve with the gifts, talents, and abilities he has given us. Pride can delude us into thinking that they are not "gifts" but spiritual merit badges that we have earned because of who "we" are. This area can create confusion at times among God's people who are confronted with the truth that a powerfully gifted person is discovered to be involved in very grotesque sin. Samson is an example of someone upon whom the Spirit would move with power right after he had spent the night with a harlot. I have heard it said that "time is the friend of truth," and the person who continues to use gifts from God while living in sin will be exposed. The Lord is so patient in waiting for us to repent when we allow sin to become rooted in our hearts. However, the day of reckoning will come if the day of repentance does not. Gifts are given; character is developed through our obedience to the Holy Spirit's guidance in our lives. We need the gifts of the Spirit wed to the fruit of the Spirit to more closely approach the desire of God for His bride.

We need a little sledgehammer work done in our hearts. The forerunner anointing can expose the religion, expose the judgment, expose the confidence in the flesh, and expose position consciousness in us. It can expose denominational pride, doctrinal pride, and spiritual giftedness pride. The forerunner anointing prepares us to purify our heart, and then we can carry this message to help prepare others. In other words, the forerunner message of repentance needs to flow out of a heart that has repented and continues to repent when sin and pride issues are brought to the light. Our prayer must me more of him and less of me until it is all of him and none of me.

A Personal Prayer

Father God, thank you for your Word, and Lord I am encouraged because you said that there is no greater man born among men than John the

Baptist, but the least in the Kingdom, is greater than John. Thank you that I am living in the Kingdom age. Thank you, Lord that the ground is level at the cross. Thank you for your grace and your mercy, oh God. Lord, I do not want religion in my heart – get it out. Please do a work in me that will allow me to have a relationship with you. Lord, I pray that you would deal with me day-by-day exposing attitudes that are wrong and forging character that will be like Christ. Thank you, Lord for John the Baptist, and thank you for this anointing – the spirit and power of Elijah that is released preparing people for your return. Thank you, Lord that it will do its work because when you come back, you are going to receive a bride to yourself that is without spot, wrinkle, blemish, or any such thing. The only one that can receive glory for having done that work will be you. So, I honor you Lord Jesus as the molder, shaper, and forger of my heart. I pray this in Jesus' wonderful, mighty, conquering, and eternal name, amen!

Chapter Ten

Wrath is on the Way!
Part One

God is a God of love and mercy; God is a God of wrath and vengeance. These two statements in the natural seemed juxtaposed. How could both be true? But they are. John the Baptizer preached passionately to his hearers saying, *"Who warned you to flee from the wrath to come?"* Part of the message the forerunner carries is a warning of the coming wrath of God, the judgment. We do not like to hear about judgment because we would much rather hear about the love and mercy of

> But when he saw many of the Pharisees and Sadducees coming to his baptism, he said to them, *"Brood of vipers! Who warned you to flee from the wrath to come?"* Matthew 3:7

God. However, we must have a balanced view of the future. Facing the future without one's hope resting solidly on Jesus is a terrifying thought.

Overcoming Fear

The forerunner must be willing to face the fear of man in order to bring people under the fear of God. The preacher who is overcome by the fear of man will have little success in causing men to be overcome by the fear of God. Jesus is coming, and just as surely as Jesus is coming, judgment is coming. Most of us had occasions when we were growing up when we got into trouble and knew that Daddy was coming home and we would have to give account for what we had done. Do you remember the dread associated with those occasions? We would have done anything to wiggle out of it and make up for it. But there was no way to undo what had been done. Praise the Lord there is a way out for us all. We have rebelled against God. We have broken His rules, yet, we can await His "homecoming" with forgiven hearts. Jesus took our wrath for us. Isn't this wonderful? Doesn't this stir a love inside of you for him?

81

Part of the forerunner message is the prophetic proclamation, not only of the coming of Jesus, but also of the coming judgment. It is interesting that John at the first coming of Christ preached about the activity of God that would be present at the second coming of Christ, the pouring out of His wrath.

The Christless Ones

Now, dear reader, know this, judgment is coming just as surely as Jesus is coming. Rather than getting too complicated about the various judgments we see reflected in Scripture, we'll deal with two main elements of judgment. Father's Heart beats with a depth of love unimaginable to us for the Christless ones. At one time, each of us was a Christless one. Eternal judgment and retribution ultimately will fall upon the Christless ones. Like those in Noah's day and in Lot's day, people are living unaware and unconcerned about the coming of the great day of God. It is the patience and forbearance of God that has kept this from already happening to all humanity. The Lord passionately waits for another and then another Christless one to become a Christlike one. The message of the cross is that God judged sin in the body of Christ. When a person receives Jesus as Savior, the judgment of their sin is taken care of through Jesus' death on the cross. They get credit for the price Jesus paid. If a person rejects Jesus, the judgment that Jesus received in their place is not credited to their account. That person will be judged and will be found wanting.

There is a coming judgment awaiting those who are not awaiting Christ. These are the lost Christless ones whom the forerunner wants to see found. These are the rebellious whom the forerunner wants to see made righteous. These are the spiritually dead who need the resurrection message preached to them. Remember every time you stand face to face with a Christless one, you are seeing the you that you used to be. All have sinned, and all need salvation. Jesus died for all. Dr. Roy Beaman, who taught the systematic theology class I had in seminary, described it this way. Jesus' death on the cross was sufficient for all to be saved; it becomes efficient to those who believe. This is true.

82

People can be saved. They can avoid the wrath that is to come. They can stand righteous before a holy God through the blood of Jesus. But they need to hear and believe; therefore we must proclaim this message to them. Eternity is a long time, and it awaits us all. It will be a Christ "filled" or a Christ "less" eternity for every human being.

The Christlike Ones

The second element of judgment has to do with the house of God or if you will, the Christlike ones. Once a person is saved the wonderful process of sanctification to conform us into the image of Christ begins. The conforming involves God dealing with all the areas in our lives that are unlike Christ. The Bible tells us that judgment must first begin in the house of God. The Bible enjoins us to examine ourselves to see whether we are in the faith. We must allow the Holy Spirit to examine us, we must examine ourselves under His scrutiny, and we must repent of the attitudes and things in our lives that are unlike Jesus Christ. Judgment must first begin with ourselves, but we must not practice the critical, judgmental, finger-pointing that so often occurs in the Body of Christ whereby we tell everybody else what is wrong with them without hearing first what is wrong with our own hearts.

The release of the forerunner anointing has to do with coming judgment, and it is a call for preparation to be judged. The Lord wants to purge His people so that they can carry a powerful message through a pure life to the lost. He wants to rid us of the religious trappings that smell of bondage. It is freedom that we offer the world. The message of liberty needs to resonate from a heart set free. Religious confinement without true freedom in Christ will turn people away from Him. The message that a forerunner carries is challenging because it shatters the religious attitudes that we have. It makes us deal with character flaws in our lives. It makes us deal with inadequacies that are revealed when we read the Scripture, and we see no reflection of Christ in our lives.

We are complete in Christ, but we are not yet completely like Christ. Repenting, obeying and submitting to the Holy Spirit as we undergo the work of sanctification, makes us more like Christ. Forerunners should be good at repenting because they cannot carry a message of repentance to others if they are not practicing daily repentance. A good repenter makes a good forerunner.

A Right View of God

Some see God only as a provider, as some kind of cosmic slot machine whose arm we pull when we want something, and think He is there to cater to our every whim and satisfy our every desire. That is a wrong view of God. We must have a balanced view. He is a God of love. He is a God of grace. He is a God of mercy. But, the Bible also presents him to be a God of wrath, a God of justice, and a God of holiness. Father is radically in love with us but His love is a jealous love. Not jealous in a sinful way, but in a righteous way. He wants us for all the right reasons. Satan wants us for all the wrong reasons.

The love of God demands that He deal with those things in our lives that are inconsistent with His love. He wants to deal with those things now so that we can stand unashamed before Him later. It is a pure Bride that Jesus will step across eternity to sweep into his passionate embrace. She will be wearing unwrinkled garments and will radiate with the glow of his glory upon her face. At that moment when he catches her in his arms, and she looks into his face, she will become like him because she will see him as he truly is. At that moment, the thoughts we have always possessed of him will be exposed as wholly inadequate and sub-standard. He will so far exceed the greatest of our most noble thoughts of him that we will not be able to refrain from releasing absolute ecstatic praise and joy from our enraptured hearts.

When God moves in judgment, He does not violate His mercy. He does not violate His grace. As a matter of fact, it is an expression of mercy, grace, and love when judgment falls. How could that be? Heaven would not be Heaven if people who were not redeemed were allowed to be there. Heaven would become like Earth is now, because that is what sin and the curse does; it spreads, like leaven spreads. It is the judgment of God that enables Heaven to be Heaven. Whom the Father loves he chastens and disciplines.

John came as a consecrated man. His parents were told by the angel that he would live a life that was separated from such things as wine and strong drink. You, by your own choice, will either be separated "from" God or separated "to" God. The forerunner is to live a life separated to God. That means becoming separated from the world and the things of the world. We use the term "worldly Christian." What does that mean? It is a phrase that identifies someone who claims to be a Christian, but when you look at them you see no evidence of Christ-like behavior, and they look just like the world. I am not talking here about immaturity issues. Immaturity is a process of growth. The Lord is always growing us from one level of maturity to another which means that he is always dealing with us about immaturity. However, if we continually refuse to grow and receive the grace God gives us to change, then our immaturity can become rebellion. When you are receiving God's grace and growing—it shows!

John bore witness of Him and cried out, saying, This was He of whom I said, 'He who comes after me is preferred before me, for He was before me.' John 1:15

When you are living for Christ and conscious of your position in Christ, it will be manifested to others. *Others* will see how the work in your life honors Christ. When people looked at John as the Messiah he ignored their praise and bore witness of Christ.

We want to look like Christ, and we can begin to do that by living a separated life and doing the Father's will. Looking like Christ comes through purity and holiness, which you cannot buy or earn. It is imputed to you directly from Christ to you. It begins to express itself through your life as a result of intimacy with God and understanding your position in Christ, and then walking in obedience to the Father.

We must have the right view of God. It cannot be like the view of the parents little Freddie had. He was talking to his friend, Susie, and said, "I'm so worried. My daddy is working twelve hours a day to make money to pay the bills. Momma, she works all day cleaning the house and cooking good meals for me." Ruthie asked, "Silly, why are you worried about it?" Freddie said, "They might escape!"

Sometimes, people have that kind of attitude about God. They think He is there just to "do for me, to do for me,– to do for me." The truth of the matter is He is the Creator. He created us for Him. True fulfillment, meaning, and significance are obtained when we start living for Him. It is not about us. It is about Him. That is part of the forerunner message. He must increase; I must decrease.

We have to have a balanced view of God. He is a God of mercy and love, but also a God of judgment. God, in his judgment is not going to say, "I am sorry; I know I said that there was a Hell, but you will not have to go there now because I am going to be merciful." Mercy is what the cross is about. Mercy is for now! Vengeance is reserved for later to those who refuse mercy.

> *Come to Me, all you who labor and are heavy laden, and I will give you rest. Matthew 11:28*
>
> *And the Spirit and the bride say, "Come!" And let him who hears say, "Come!" And let him who thirsts come. Whoever desires, let him take the water of life freely. Revelation 22:17*

Today, there is an invitation to come to the cross. The invitation comes from Jesus, the Holy Spirit and the church in Revelation. But there will be a time when the invitation will no longer be issued. There will be a time when instead of the "Come!" message, the message will be "Depart from me. Go! Go away to the place prepared for the devil and his angels." Right now the invitation is to come, and we prepare for Jesus' coming. Those who do not accept the invitation will not be saved. When he returns, judgment will await them. Once the eternal transaction of salvation occurs you can rest in the finished work of the cross to escape wrath while receiving the loving discipline of a loving Father who has adopted you into His forever family.

A Personal Prayer

Oh Holy God, my Father, Thank you for saving me from the wrath to come. Help me to hide in my heart a urgency to help others to flee from the wrath that is to come. Please forgive me for the times that I have walked by the lost without considering where they are headed. Help me to be a witness for you. I desire to be used to point people to the place of rescue. Fill me anew and afresh with your Holy Spirit that I might be a powerful witness for Christ. I pray this in Jesus name, amen.

Chapter Eleven

Wrath is on the Way!
Part Two

Eschatology in the Scripture tells us that Jesus is coming back in second coming glory, and the Earth is going to be exposed to the wrath of God. We have not been appointed to wrath.

> Eschatology (Greek) Last. The term refers to the 'doctrine of the last things'.

We are protected from wrath through the blood of Jesus. In the Old Testament, God told Noah to prepare for the coming deluge by building an ark. Noah built the ark, and then God poured his judgment out on the Earth and Noah was safe inside the Ark. In the New Testament, that ark is Christ. Just like the children of Israel in Egypt were protected from death by the covering of blood in the Old Testament (Exodus 12:13), so are we. In the New Testament, the blood that covers us is the blood Jesus shed on the cross. We are safe from the judgment of God that will be poured out on this Earth when we are in Christ. The forerunner wants as many people as possible safely covered by the powerful blood of Jesus, therefore they will warn people of the coming wrath.

Who warned you to escape the wrath to come?[Q] The wrath is on

> For the Son of Man will come in the glory of His Father with His angels, and then He will reward each according to his works.
> Matthew 16:27

the way. As a matter of fact, the wrath of God is already being poured out against sin in the Earth. God's wrath is poured out at the same time you engage in sin. Romans 1:18 tells us that sin carries with it the wrath of God. When you sin, there is judgment inherent in that sin. Even as believers in Christ we will still be held accountable for how we live and what we have accomplished. Our salvation is complete in what Jesus did on the cross, but there will be the

---

[Q] *Do you remember someone who warned **you** of the wrath to come? Do you remember the words that were used?*

Bema--the judgment of believers, as foretold in 2 Corinthians 5.

Even as a believer, if you do not hear the message of the Lord and prepare and receive what God wants to do, it can cause you to be in a situation of shame when you stand before the judgment seat of Christ. What we do now will affect us then. Judgment is a sure thing.

> He who flees from the fear shall fall into the pit, And he who gets out of the pit shall be caught in the snare.
> Jeremiah 48:44

The Fearless Forerunner

The Bible tells us that the fear of man brings a snare. When you run in fear, you jump out of the kettle into the frying pan. A forerunner is not afraid to warn people of the wrath to come, not in a mean and vindictive way, but with a broken heart. The forerunner asks "What will you say when you stand before God?" We *will* stand before God and give an account of our lives. The fear of God in the forerunner protects him from the snare of the fear of man. I heard Oswald Chambers wrote that if you find a man who fears man, he will fear everything else, but if you find a man who fears only God, he will fear nothing else. Intimidation and fear are weapons the enemy constantly uses to back down God's people. This was Goliath's strategy against the armies of Israel until the day that young David came with a sling in his hand and the fear of God in his heart. He knew that God would back him up if he refused to allow Goliath to back him down.

> ...scoffers will come in the last days, walking according to their own lusts, and saying, "Where is the promise of His coming? ...The Lord is not slack concerning His promise, as some count slackness, but is longsuffering toward us, not willing that any should perish but that all should come to repentance.
> 2 Peter 3:3-4, 9

Judgment is coming. Jesus tells us in Matthew 25:41 that Hell was not prepared for people. People will enter Hell because they have listened to the voice of Satan instead of the voice of God. When Satan came into the Garden of Eden he convinced Eve to make the wrong choice. She, through deception, chose to believe that she would not die as God said she would if she ate from the tree of knowledge of good and evil. She disobeyed God and ate, then Adam ate, and ultimately they died. What God said came to pass. Peter warns us about doubting the coming judgment and gives us insight into the reasons Jesus has not come back yet. One reason is that the bride is getting ready and prepared. The other reason is that He does not want people to perish. It is His mercy that has delayed the second coming. He is not willing that anybody should perish because He knows after the second coming there will only be judgment.

> *His winnowing fan is in His hand, and He will thoroughly clean out His threshing floor, and gather His wheat into the barn; but He will burn up the chaff with unquenchable fire."*
> Matthew 3:12
>
> *... and they were judged, each one according to his works. And anyone not found written in the Book of Life was cast into the lake of fire.*
> Revelation 20: 13, 15
>
> *And the smoke of their torment ascends forever and ever; and they have no rest day or night.*
> Revelation 14:11

John the Baptist carried the message, "Flee from the wrath to come." In Matthew 3, John warns of the fire that is awaiting those who suffer the wrath of God. Revelation 20 warns us of the consequences of being judged after death. Revelation 14:11 makes it clear that no rest day or night is a condition of Hell. Today, the word goes forth, "Come unto me and I will give you rest," but then there will be no rest day nor night if you do not know Jesus Christ.

Jesus says in Matthew 10:28 "And do not fear those who kill the body but cannot kill the soul. But rather fear Him who is able to destroy both soul and body in Hell." How can a God that is loving and merciful banish people to Hell? Now people abide under God's grace and mercy because He sent His Son to die for them. Jesus was the propitiation for our sins, literally the mercy seat. The cross is the place where the blood was sprinkled. It is a picture of

> Propitiation
> To gain or regain the favor or good will of.
> In the Old Testament, blood had to be shed – something had to die or be sacrificed – to ward off the wrath of God that was incurred when a person sinned.

wrath and bloodshed being applied as a covering. Jesus became our mercy seat. The wrath of God that we deserve was poured out on Jesus,

90

and when you trust Jesus then you are under the covering of mercy and protected from the wrath.

Everything that can be done for you to save you from Hell has been done. If a person has not accepted Jesus Christ as their Savior, they will not be able to blame God for their condition in Hell. Today, there is an invitation to come to Christ and to know one's name is recorded in the Lamb's book of life, but someday there will be no opportunity. The forerunner knows this and wants to get the message to all the nations and to every soul on planet earth. There is a sense of responsibility that the forerunner carries to spread the good news that people can be saved and escape the wrath that is on the way. If you are not saved, I bid you, give your heart to Christ.

God's Passion toward You

Thank God if you are saved. If you are saved then you will be given notice by the Holy Spirit of areas that need to be changed in your life. He will faithfully contend for all of your heart's passion to be focused on the beautiful Son of God. He will hover over you with a holy jealousy that says, "You belong to Christ." The Lord's love is lavished upon us and His heart beats with joy as He thinks of us. He wants us and the very wanting of his heart for us is an amazing truth to me. His love carries a fire in it that is fanned into flame against anything and everything that arises to cool our hearts toward Christ. His fiery love for us will cause us to have a fiery love for Him. His love reproduces itself in our hearts. As it gains momentum inside of us, it casts away all the fear that causes us to run from Him instead of to Him. Think of God's judgments in this way. The judgments of God will ultimately eliminate everything that refuses to submit to the love of God. Love will endure for eternity, and love will never fail because God is love.

God does take sin seriously regardless of where it is found. If you think being saved means that you can deliberately dabble in sin without any response from God, you may want to read First Corinthians again, especially the part where people died because of their abuse of the Lord's table. It is important to understand that we are

91

accountable to the Lord for motives and wrong actions that flow out of wrong motives.

The Reality of Hell

The stark truth is that there is a Hell whose belly is burning and awaiting those who die without making Christ the king of their lives. It is a literal place where literal people will go who do not know Christ. It is a place of outer

> Then He will also say to those on the left hand, 'Depart from Me, you cursed, into the everlasting fire prepared for the devil and his angels.' Matthew 25:41

darkness where the worm dies not, where there is weeping and gnashing of teeth. It is a place where people go who refuse to be separated to God and chose to live separated from God.

Paul says, "Knowing therefore the terror of the Lord, we persuade men." (2 Corinthians 5:11) May God birth in you a conviction to tell your family members who do not know Christ, your work associates who do not know Christ, and your neighbors who do not know Christ, that there is wrath coming. Tell them about the escape hatch whose name is Jesus. We have been commissioned to do just that, and it is part of the forerunner's message.

> For he who eats and drinks in an unworthy manner eats and drinks judgment to himself, not discerning the Lord's body. For this reason many are weak and sick among you, and many sleep. For if we would judge ourselves, we would not be judged. But when we are judged, we are chastened by the Lord, that we may not be condemned with the world.
> 1 Corinthians 11:29-32

The forerunner challenges people to escape the wrath that is to come. There is a time limit on the mercy of God, and there will be a time when God will demand justice.

No one will escape judgment. The penalty of sin is death. When you come to Christ, you are offering yourself for His judgment. You are asking God to judge your sins through what happened to Jesus on the cross. Christ died on the cross for you because He received the judgment of death and the judgment of eternal separation for you. He cleanses us from sin.

When Eve was deceived, she must have thought that she would not die. She must have thought she was not going to be judged. She must have thought there was not a Hell. Dear reader, it does not matter what you believe about Hell. It will not change the fact of what God has ordained and decreed. You need to make sure your belief system is in line with what God says in His Word because it is a sure word that is settled forever in the Heaven.

There is a liberal theology in our day that denies Hell. There is another theology that teaches the doctrine of total annihilation. Neither is what the Bible teaches. The Word of God teaches that people who die without Christ in their lives will go to a literal place, and they will have a conscious awareness. Jesus tells us in Chapter 16 of Luke that the rich man in Hell recognized Lazarus the beggar and Abraham from afar.[Q] Souls in Hell will have cognitive ability to recognize people. They will have the ability to regret. They will understand lost opportunity. They will be cast into outer darkness. There will be extreme, utter isolation. It will be a place of unquenchable fire and punishment.

> Many will say to Me in that day, 'Lord, Lord, have we not prophesied in Your name, cast out demons in Your name, and done many wonders in Your name?' And then I will declare to them, 'I never knew you; depart from Me, you who practice lawlessness!'
> Matthew 7:22-23

If you do not know Christ and you understand what Hell really is, if you do not get scared, then something is wrong! The Holy Spirit will convict you and cause you to realize that you need to know the terror of the Lord. You need to be persuaded to come to Christ. The fear of the Lord is the beginning of knowledge and wisdom. When you come under His covering, you do not have to live in fear. He awaits the opportunity to express His love as Heavenly Father to every lost soul. He has already commended His love to us by refusing to spare His only Son for us. The Lord has provided a way for humanity; He awaits their response. The blood of the cross and long since dried, but, its power to save remains.

[Q] *What is the significance of this passage in light of those who teach that all identity will be lost in eternity? It will be personal then, it should be now.*

93

Meaningless Ministry

Being saved does not mean that your name is on the roll of the church down the road, that you have been faithful in tithing, that you read the Bible, and that you have not missed a church service in a long time. Those things are just religious activities if you do not know Jesus. Do not be fooled into thinking that religious activity will assure you a place with God in eternity. If you have not allowed Him to birth eternity in your heart and give you everlasting life, if you have not repented of your sins and embraced the cross and the Christ of the cross, if you have not allowed Jesus to become Lord of your life, then you will not spend eternity with God.

Understand the subtle power of deception. You can be engaged in ministry, you can use the name of Jesus, you can lay hands on and pray for people, you can cast out devils, and you can still never know Christ. Jesus warned the people not to be deceived about religious activity, as the Pharisees and Sadducees had been.

Judgment is coming. Search your heart. If you know you are genuinely saved, the Holy Spirit will bear witness with your spirit. I know I am saved because my spirit bears witness with the Holy Spirit, and the Holy Spirit bears witness with my spirit. If you examine yourself and all you find is religious activity, and there is no relationship with Jesus Christ, make things right with God. If you are without Christ, I plead with you; flee from the wrath that is to come. If you know Christ and you are not living right, allow God to do all in your life that He desires to do for you to glorify Him!

God is not mocked. When you know Christ, there is evidence of a changed life. Knowing Christ does not mean that you are without fault in any regard, It does not mean that you will be fully mature, but it does mean you will

> Therefore, if anyone is in Christ, he is a new creation; old things have passed away; behold, all things have become new.
> 2 Corinthians 5:17

be changed. Paul tells us in Second Corinthians that all things will become new. You will be more like Jesus, and if you are living right, you will become more like Jesus the longer you live. The older we get, the more like Christ we ought to be.

Have you been working arm in arm with people for weeks, months, maybe years, and you have never shared Christ? God help us to understand what awaits them across the threshold of death. Do you have family members who don't know Christ, and you have not witnessed to them? Have you been faithful to share Jesus with your children?Q It can be very hard to talk to family members about Christ, but do you understand what the Bible teaches about where they will spend eternity if they do not know Christ? I am not trying to take you on a guilt trip, but reminding you of the seriousness of the trip that everyone will take after they breathe their last breath.

Jesus is coming. Bless his name! And, judgment is coming. You have been given one life to live; it can be used to resound the glory of God or it can be lived selfishly. Which way are you living it? You have been given the Holy Spirit, the Word of God, the anointing to be used of the Lord in this Earth. What are you doing?

Are you living in light of the truth of judgment? Are you responding to others in the light that they will experience judgment in their lives? The forerunner will be out front with a message borne by love that says, "Wrath is on the way! Flee to the cross of Jesus Christ!"

It is so important that we carry the Lord's passion for the lost. I do not remember all the times that I have obeyed the Lord and led someone to Christ, but I vividly remember the times when I refused to obey with grievous results. While working construction in the mid- 80's, there was an occasion that the Spirit strongly prompted me to go to the hospital and witness to a man with whom I had been working. Instead of going by the hospital after work, I went home thinking I would make the visit the following afternoon. After all, he wasn't in serious condition. He had been working beside me everyday for months. That night, the man died. I cannot tell you the sinking feeling that filled my soul as a result of my failure to heed the voice of God.

Q *When is the last time you shared Christ with someone?*

A couple of years later on a Saturday morning, the Spirit spoke strongly to me to visit a lady in the community where I was pastoring and witness to her. I did not go. I thought I would go in a few days when it was more convenient. The next afternoon as I drove by her house on the way to our evening worship service, I thought about stopping by and making the visit so I could check it off my list. It was close to church time so I went on to service. In a little while the message was delivered to our church service that the lady had just dropped dead at home. It was totally unexpected. She had not even been sick. This was the second time I had quenched and ignored the voice of the Spirit with tragic consequences. I hope that there will never be a third.

As forerunners we must be faithful to proclaim to people what Jesus is going to do once he comes back. John the Baptist faithfully proclaimed what Jesus would do once he arrived at his first coming; we must be faithful to declare what he is going to do upon his arrival when he comes in second coming glory.

A Personal Prayer

Father, please forgive me for my complacency, my smugness, and my satisfaction. Forgive me, Lord, for the sin of silence and prayerlessness. Oh God, may I hear the forerunner message calling me to repent, to change, and to live in light of judgment. Oh Father God, I pray for your conviction to fall and to break up the fallow ground in my heart, break down the walls in mind, and do business Lord in the corridors of my heart. I desire to have a pure heart toward you and a passionate heart toward the Christless ones. In Jesus' name, amen!

Chapter Twelve

The U-Turn Message

Another aspect of the forerunner anointing is that it calls for change and preparation. Remember in Matthew 3:1 we are told that John the Baptist came preaching in the wilderness of Judea saying, "Repent. Repent, for the Kingdom of God is at hand." You can identify the forerunner anointing because of the message that it carries; it's time to change! No more business as usual! Things are shifting! Things have to be brought into alignment! Things have to be made right! Repent, for the Kingdom of God is at hand! Jesus carried the same message when he walked the earth (Matthew 4:17 and Luke 13:3).

> From that time Jesus began to preach and to say, "Repent, for the kingdom of Heaven is at hand." Matthew 4:17
>
> I tell you, no; but unless you repent you will all likewise perish. Luke 13:3

Metanoia is the Greek word for repentance. It means to make an about face, a 180° turn, a change of mind. It indicates a person who is living and thinking one way and turns and starts living and thinking the opposite way. When you are confronted with the truth of God and it spins you around and you move in the opposite way with a new set of values, you have experienced true repentance.

> Metanoia (Greek) Repentance; change of mind which results in change of lifestyle.

When the forerunner anointing comes upon a person, they begin to challenge and confront people with the truth of God to bring about conviction and repentance that will yield itself in change. This change will help usher in the restoration that God has ordained. It moves from one heart to other hearts through changed lives. Much change in the human heart is necessary to get us to the place where God can trust us with what He has ordained for us. The forerunner anointing calls for change and preparation. It is a change that gets things in order so that

97

we can be involved in what God is doing. All of us need to accept the fact that there are things about us that need to be changed. Not everybody is going to receive the call for change, not everybody is going to hear it. You can be right in the middle of a move of God, and it may not move you because you are not willing to receive the truth.

Is anybody completely like Jesus? Of course we are positionally by faith, but I am not talking about in faith. I am not talking about in the mind of God. I am talking about in daily lifestyle. We are not completely like him in a practical, functional sense. Is anyone perfect, just like Jesus? Maybe for a few fleeting moments people may see a reflection of Him in our lives. But until He returns and we see Him as He is, we will not be absolutely, completely like Him. We will be changing from glory to glory. We should become more like Jesus as we allow the Holy Spirit to lead us. We are complete in Him, but we are not yet completely like Him.[Q] The forerunner anointing calls for change that will help us to be more like Jesus.

> *Beloved, now we are children of God; and it has not yet been revealed what we shall be, but we know that when He is revealed, we shall be like Him, for we shall see Him as He is.*
> *1 John 3:2*

Remember when you used to court – to date? You would probably make sure everything was just right as you would get ready to go out with your sweetheart. I remember as an eighteen year old on Saturday, I would drive 51 miles one way to see my sweetheart. On Saturday, I got out the water hose, the bucket, the sponge, the car cleaner and the wax. I made my little yellow 1971 Volkswagen Beetle shine. You could see those orange flames on the side sparkling. I vacuumed that orange shag carpet I had personally installed on the inside. I made sure the seven speakers I had strategically located throughout that big car were working. I had that car ready. I was ready to show up and impress my special somebody.I would put on my bell bottoms, my platform shoes, my double-knit shirt, my leather choker,

---

[Q]*What is in your life that you think is keeping you from being completely like Jesus? How do you think the Lord would like you to deal with it?*

and I would style my hair just right. That was the day of the afro, and I had the best one in my town. With my afro poofed and my car shined, I would head off to visit my sweetheart. I was a forerunner because I was the first boy in my school to have an afro! I wanted to make a good impression. I knew I was about to see somebody special. I got ready, I really got ready! It worked too! We eventually married, and we both have experienced a lot of change since then. I am now afro-less but I am still forerunning.

Spiritually, the forerunner anointing causes us to be motivated in such a way. We want to be ready to be in the presence of our King. We want to have everything just right so that He will be pleased with us, not so that He will accept us, but because we love Him, and we know He loves us and we just want everything to be right when we are with Him. The forerunner anointing enables us to be motivated to prepare, to change, to get things right, and to be prepared for our Lord and whatever He may require of us.

Remember, a forerunner is a person who is prepared in order to prepare the people to prepare for the Lord. A forerunner will first be prepared by the Lord himself. John, even in his mother's womb, experienced the hand of the Lord on his little life influencing him toward destiny. Then, through years in the wilderness, the Lord continued preparing John to be a preparer of the people. The Lord loves to deal and work with people in obscure places, mold them into someone who can carry the life message that he is giving them, and then release them. When God puts his mighty hand under somebody and beings to lift them up, there is no power in Hell that can stop that. When you start being exalted by the mighty hand of God, nothing is going to stop that process because God opens the door that no man can close. And, when He closes a door, no man can open it.

Forerunners carry the spirit of Elijah, and can be radical, non-mainstream, and different. You may be from an obscure place nobody has ever heard of, but you are carrying the message of truth that is burning in you. One forerunner may not look like another forerunner, but there are certain characteristics that are common to all forerunners.

The forerunner looks for evidence of life and fruit. They are not interested in relics that carry the dust of inactivity. They abide by the old saying that says, "When the horse is dead, dismount."

In Matthew 3, John tells the religious people of the day that there must be change in their lives if they want to be part of what God is doing. He is telling us there needs to be some evidence of change in our lives. There needs to be an about face: living for the devil, turn around and live for God;

> Therefore bear fruits worthy of repentance…
> Matthew 3:8

living for the world, turn around and live for God; living in the flesh, turn around and follow the Spirit. That is repentance.

The forerunner is looking for evidence of life and fruit. If it is not producing, kill it. If it is not working, change it. If it is not getting the job done, scrap it. When you get that radical "go for God" attitude, nothing else matters. Get the junk out of the way, find what God is doing, and join in because that is what is going to bear fruit. Of course, it is important that the fruit of the Spirit in one's own life not be discarded due to a zeal to tear down dead traditions to raise a true altar of worship to the Lord.

There ought to be some evidence that there is the blessing of God on what is being done. It is not about doing something and asking God to bless it. It is about seeking the heart of God, finding out what He wants done, and then taking the steps of obedience and faith to see it done. He will then bless what you are doing. Faithful is He who has

> He who calls you is faithful, who also will do it. 1 Thessalonians 5:24

called you, who will also do it. Even in the ministry of Jesus, He understood that what was being accomplished was being accomplished by the Spirit, by His Father. Too often we are guilty of wanting God to rubber stamp our plans. We have good intentions but are guilty of wrong inventions. We make the order and then want God to pay for it. It cannot be overemphasized how important it is for us to be led by the Holy Spirit. This is the key to success. He will always have us where we need to be, doing what we need to do, when we need to be doing it. His plans are much better than our puny brainstorms.

Whatever it Takes to Obey

Missionary Bobby Gibson works in the remote areas of Honduras. In late 2003, he wanted to visit a people he had heard of called the Mosquito Indians, some of whom had never seen a North American. He knew he would have to travel in a small boat down a river to find the people who lived in houses on stilts. After several failed attempts get a boat to journey on the river to reach the Mosquito Indians, he and Dr. Jorge who speaks Spanish, once again went to the river and were finally able to get a boat. They traveled down the river looking for the houses on stilts. On the way, they met a man who was able to take them where they wanted to go, and finally they came to a village where there were about 12 houses together. They started ministering to the people who lived there. Bobby Gibson has that forerunner spirit of going into those places that have not been visited.

> *The words that I speak to you I do not speak on My own authority; but the Father who dwells in Me does the works.*
> *John 14:10*

They stayed the night in the village of the Mosquito Indians who have British, Spanish, and African heritage. They have their own language. While there, Bobby would preach in English. Doctor Jorge would translate what Bobby said into Spanish, and another man would translate it from Spanish into the Mosquito language. Can you imagine listening to a preacher who would have to stop after every sentence,... who would have to stop after every sentence,... who would have to stop after every sentence,... and wait,... and wait,... and wait,... for it to be translated?... for it to be translated?... for it to be translated? The word was spoken in three different languages, and forty-five people were saved! The forerunner wants to be the first one there, to be the first one to declare the message of God or the new fresh word of the Lord to a people. The work of the forerunner is after true God produced fruit.

The forerunner does not give up. He continues to pursue his work because he has heard from God. He knows what God has said. He knows what God wants to do and he will take no other option and receive no excuses because God has spoken. John had heard the voice of

God. He heard the words of the prophet Isaiah saying "Prepare the way of the Lord." He knew the message he was to carry and when the people came and asked him who he was, he said, "I am a voice crying in the wilderness. Prepare ye the way of the Lord." He knew what he had heard God speak in his hearing. He knew what he was supposed to do. He was not going to back down to religion. He was going to keep preaching what God had told him to preach. He also saw the evidence of the fruit it was bearing. People were coming out and they were being changed. They were undergoing a baptism unto repentance.

In other words, there was an outward demonstration that they were going to change and prepare their hearts to receive the Messiah because of John's message. Then one day John pointed to Jesus and told his helpers, "Behold, the Lamb of God. He takes away the sins of the world." The next day, they followed Jesus. He knew what the message was that God had given him to carry. It was not the message of the Pharisees or the Sadducees or the Scribes. It was not the message that had been carried by his father, grandfather, and great-grandfather. God had moved upon him with a fresh anointing as a forerunner to prepare for the next visitation of God.

The forerunner John explained to the people who came to see him that if they were going to be a part of the new wineskin and shift, that they would have to change and show some evidence of change. John gave a very, very strong word. He was looking for fruit. He was interested in works that produce.

A Personal Prayer

Father, forgive me for taking trips down dead-end alleys. Please forgive me for taking off on my own without receiving instructions from you. Help me to stay on course. May the U-turn be seen in my life at any time that I have missed the leading of your Holy Spirit. I desire to do whatever it takes to obey you. I surrender to your plans and purposes for my life. I bless you for all the times you have moved upon my heart in convicting power. Thank you for loving me enough to discipline me. I love you Father and I pray this in Jesus' name, amen.

Chapter Thirteen

The Ax Anointing

> *He has promised, saying, "Yet once more I shake not only the earth, but also Heaven." Now this, "Yet once more," indicates the removal of those things that are being shaken, as of things that are made, that the things which cannot be shaken may remain.*
> Hebrews 12: 26-27

Are you frustrated and restless? In this season, there is a lot of restlessness and frustration throughout the body of Christ because a lot of people are tired of going through the motions, doing the same things that they have always done and getting the same results, and not seeing any fruit or life. That frustration and restlessness, I believe, is an indication of the forerunner spirit that is stirring people up because they are hungry to see life. They are hungry to see fruit and something working in the Kingdom.

As the name of one of C. Peter Wagner's books indicates, there is a "Churchquake" taking place. In the last three verses of Hebrews Chapter Twelve, we are told that God is going to shake everything that can be shaken so that which remains cannot be shaken. That is what is happening. God is shaking all the dead stuff loose. God is shaking it loose so that what remains is of Him. John goes on to tell us that any tree that does not bear good fruit should be cut down and thrown into the fire. John was looking for fruit that is in keeping with repentance.

We all want the "Acts" anointing that fell on the disciples in the early church, but do we want the *"ax"* anointing that accompanies

> *And even now the ax is laid to the root of the trees. Therefore every tree which does not bear good fruit is cut down and thrown into the fire.*
> Matthew 3: 10-11

the forerunner call to fall on our lives? John's message tells us that if we are going to prepare for the Lord, we had better get ready for the ax anointing to be turned loose on our lives.[Q1] The dead stuff is

---

[Q1] *Are you ready to be trimmed? Where do you think the Lord will begin first in your life?*

going to go. If it is not producing, God is going to kill it. Across the body of Christ there needs to be a lot of killings. *Please do not shut this book until you hear me out!* We need to slaughter a lot of sacred cows – issues that are dividing churches that have nothing to do with church and that are building walls in the Kingdom. John the Baptist, the forerunner said, "The ax is laid to the root." The Spirit of Elijah, as it were, causes the ax head to float to the surface again and equips the forerunner to use it. No more flailing away with handles with no heads.

Of course, remember, the one who is prepared by the Lord to prepare the people to prepare for the Lord is first prepared. So before you get out the ax and start toward your neighbor's house, you must start in your own front and back yard.[Q2] If it is not bringing forth fruit, if it is not going to use God's good soil, God's good sun, God's good water, to make a seed sprout, then it's root must be cut. The man or woman, who would carry a sharp ax for the Lord, must first have its sharp edge cut into the depths of his or her own soul.

If all we are doing is trimming limbs, we are going to continue to struggle. It is when the ax is laid to the root that the bad trees in the yard are dealt with permanently so the good trees can grow and receive all the available sun, soil, fertilizer, and water. That is the purpose of the ax anointing -- to enable us to examine ourselves daily and to eliminate anything in our lives that is not producing fruit for the Lord. Then we can lay it to the roots among the barren trees growing in the orchard of the church.

This examination does not need to be just once a day. I would encourage you pray to allow the Holy Spirit to help you achieve awareness in your life that will enable you to know immediately when you step out of bounds. The first moment

> Lord, show me my heart. Examine my heart. Have I said something today that I should not have said? Lord, have I loved my brother and my sister the way I should have loved them? Have I done this day what I am responsible before you to do? Lord, has there been anything in my thought-life that is not holy and pure?

[Q2] *Is there something God wants you to put to death in your life? He has a sharp ax!*

that you become aware of sin is the first moment that you need to deal with it. If you are going to live as a forerunner and develop as a forerunner then you will carry a message of repentance, and you must live a lifestyle of change and repentance. It does very little good for us to confront people and challenge people to change if we are not changing ourselves.

Is there any sin in your life that you refuse to put to death? If so, that is where you will find the heart of your struggle. Ask this question every day, "Am I changing, and in what way?" As you go to sleep at night, ask "Lord, in what way have you changed me today?" In the physical and in the natural your body is constantly changing. In the spirit we ought to be changing, and being moved from one level of glory to the next level of glory. The Bible says we are being changed from one level of glory to the next level of glory. It is often repentance that is the key that will open the door for you to step across the threshold into the next realm of God's glory in your life.

If we are being changed, and repentance is necessary for change, then it is repentance that is the launching pad for you to journey to the next level of glory. Moving to the next level of glory means that you are becoming more like Christ. The fullness of glory is when you behold the face of Jesus Christ, the glory of God. When you repent, you are becoming more like Jesus. Adam was made in God's image and now the restoration, through the spirit of God, of that image is being offered to us so that we can become more and more like Jesus Christ. God predestined and ordained this conformation (Romans 8:29). I know that this is repetitive and you have already heard this in this book. But I do this purposely. Conformity to Christ is the grand goal of God's purposes in our lives here. It is through dying to self and becoming wholly abandoned to him that we see the manifestation of his likeness in

> *For whom He foreknew, He also predestined to be conformed to the image of His Son.*
> *Romans 8:29*

our lives. Sometimes we try to change without repentance, and that just causes frustration. Sometimes we try to change everybody around us, but *we* do not want to change. It will be repentance that enables us to

105

step into the next realm of the glory of God. We have all fallen short of the glory of God. It is repentance that enables us to turn back to the place that Adam left and experience more of the fullness of God in our lives. Adam and Eve were in the glory of God. They started listening to the serpent's voice, and they moved away from God. We bear that Adamic nature of listening to the voice of the serpent, and we have to come to a point in our lives where we turn away from that voice and turn back to God. That is repentance, the message of the forerunner, and what God wants to bring into the Earth will not happen until we repent and change.

A Lifestyle of Repentance

A lot of times when we ask God to come, God is waiting on us to repent! Repentance is a gift. God grants repentance to His people. It is something that God does for us that enables us to change, to step into His glory from which Adam fell. So do not be ashamed to repent; be ashamed if you do not. We need to live a lifestyle of repentance. I am not talking about living life with a shovel in your hand so that you can dig up the past and dwell on how bad you were. I am talking about developing a sensitivity to the Holy Spirit that yields and changes at the slightest mention by the Spirit. Don't confuse this either with a pseudo-spiritual superiority that causes people to live apart from the God's call to reach the world. The answer is not living in a monastery; the answer is that Christ is living in you. He is with you wherever you go and will empower you to be an agent of change in a corrupt world without becoming corrupted by the world. This is what he did. We need seasons of drawing aside and a lifestyle of drawing aside. Very often, this is essential for us to kill the hold the world has on us. There is a difference in drawing aside to behold his beauty and stepping aside to keep from seeing the world. The Pharisees stepped aside from the world but never drew aside to really see the Lord. If they had they would have recognized him when he stood face to face with them. They were

> If you think you are not sinning, just go ahead and practice repenting anyway!

blinded to his beauty because they were too busy beholding their own "righteousness." While they avoided the tide of the world outside it was drowning them on the inside.

When John the Baptist came out of the wilderness, he had been living a lifestyle of repentance. He had turned away from the ways of the world. He had turned away from the ways of religion. He left all behind to carry the message of repentance. He allowed God to shape, mold, and fashion him, so he could then share that message with others. In his time apart from the world he did become conformed to the Lord. When Jesus showed up he had no difficulty recognizing who he really was. This is how we tell if our "aside times" are working. We learn to discern the presence and the beauty of the Lord. Repentance helps remove the veils that blind us to the beauty of our King.

More Like Jesus

If we are not being conformed to the Lord, we are not on track. When we are without repentance and are trying to carry the message of the forerunner, we will often do more damage than good. We are swinging an ax handle without an ax head! We might bruise a lot of people, but we will not cut any roots.

It is out of the lifestyle of repentance that the message can flow with anointing, authority, and love that causes the hearts of men and women to become convicted so that they want to change. It so important, so very, very important, that we have a time daily during which we ask the Lord to show us where we need to change. However, be happy He does not show us all at once everything that needs changing. It would be overwhelming! We can be happy when we attend the funeral of another wrong attitude, another wrong habit, and another wrong motive. This lifelong journey to the graveyard will continue until we see him and become like him because we see him as he is. This daily dying will keep us experiencing his daily living in and through our lives.

The church must carry a message that will turn people back to God. As the forerunner anointing is released and the church receives it, then the church begins changing and looking more like Jesus and walking more in the same authority and anointing that John carried, which was the spirit and power of Elijah. What happened in the ministry of John and Jesus, people coming to see the truth that was alive, will begin to happen in the church of today. There will be good fruit; there will be evidence that God has visited. The original command that God gave us was to be fruitful, multiply, and fill the Earth. The forerunner is looking for fruit because being fruitful is in alignment with God's original design.

Dead Works

There are some questions that need to be asked to determine if a church is a forerunner church and carrying the message God wants her to carry. The answers to the questions should show evidence of fruit worthy of repentance.

- Are people being saved?
- Are people from the nations being saved?
- Are people being baptized?
- Are people being taught daily to follow Christ?
- Is the evidence of the fruit of the spirit being seen in the members' lives?

Dead works abound, but dead works make good firewood at the altar of God. What are dead works? Here is one little list I ran across. It is just religious activity, such as jumping on the bandwagon, wading through paperwork, running around in circles, pushing your luck, spinning your wheels, adding fuel to the fire, beating your head against the wall, climbing the walls, beating your own drum, dragging your heels, jumping to conclusions, grasping at straws, fishing for compliments, throwing your weight around, and passing the buck.

> If being a Christian were declared to be a crime, would there be enough evidence to convict you as guilty? Is there fruit in your life? Is there fruit and evidence in your life of Christ likeness?

Too often in the past we who are the church have been too quick to imitate what God is doing for someone else instead of allowing the

108

Lord to do what He wants to do through us. How many times has the anointing lifted off what God had been blessing because the focus shifted to packaging what God was doing so that it could reproduced somewhere else. I am not suggesting that we should not learn and glean from what God is doing in other places through other people. We can and we should endeavor to glean and learn. We must, however, avoid the danger of looking to a system or structure to deliver what can only be delivered by the power of the Holy Spirit. The Lord is jealous of His glory. Methods and structures change and are necessary but they are futile without the Spirit breathing upon them. It is about where our focus is and who is getting the glory. Dead works are those things that suck the life out of us without replenishing or renewing us. Where there is life, the reaping will follow the sowing, and there will be fruit to show for work that has been initiated and blessed by God. To do things because we have always done them is redundant, thoughtless, and often dead. Being led is much preferred to being dead. The Spirit ever leads us through death to self into the life of Christ. Dead works keep us busy maintaining our cemeteries, making sure our well manicured graves are not disturbed by someone carrying resurrection power.

A Personal Prayer

Oh Lord, my Father, lay the ax to the root of dead works in my life. Help me to see and abandon those efforts, works, and areas of my life that are fruitless. Transform the barren areas of my life into areas that are productive for your Kingdom's purposes. Forgive me for asking you to breathe on things that need to be buried. Forgive me for expending my energies on things that will never bring you glory. I desire to be fruitful in every area of my life. Deepen my understanding of what it means to live in the fullness of your grace. May my work really be Christ working in and through me for your honor and glory. In Jesus' name, amen.

Chapter Fourteen

Power and Purity

> *He will baptize you with the Holy Spirit and fire.*
> *Matthew 3:11*

Forerunners need to encourage the baptism of the Holy Spirit and the baptism of fire. We need to lovingly let people know that it is important to be baptized in the Holy Spirit and fire. He will baptize *you* with the Holy Spirit and with fire. We like to talk about the experience of the baptism of the Holy Spirit. It is *wonderful*! But commensurate with that message is the baptism of fire, which can be a wonderfully painful experience. It is Jesus who is the baptizer.

The Forerunner of All Forerunners

John was declaring that Jesus would be able to do something for you that no man can do. A person can baptize you in water, but only Jesus can baptize you in the Holy Spirit and in fire. John understood that; he understood his portion, and he understood the Lord's portion. John baptized people in water, but he knew that the Savior who was coming after him was mightier than he was.

> *John bore witness of Him and cried out, saying, "This was He of whom I said, 'He who comes after me is preferred before me, for He was before me.'*
> *John 1:15*

John understood even though he was a forerunner, there was a forerunner that foran him, and His name was Jesus. Jesus is the forerunner of all forerunners. John knew the portion he carried in being the forerunner that God called him to be was to baptize in water. But, there was another forerunner preferred before John, and even though He was before John, He would come after John, and follow up on John's work of baptism with water. He was going to baptize with the Holy Spirit, and He was going to baptize with fire. He did come and the baptism of the spirit and fire commenced. Jesus cleans us out and gets the chaff out of our lives. When He comes back to get us, He will fill Daddy God's barns with good, chaff-free, tare-free wheat.

A Winning Combination

There is a balance between the baptism of the Holy Spirit and the baptism of fire. One has to do with power, and the other has to do with purity. It is important to have the winning combination of the two. If you have power received through the baptism of the Holy Spirit, but you are impure, then you are going to damage people and damage the Kingdom. Exciting things may happen, and there may be some flashy fireworks, but they are going to fizzle to a dud before long. The baptism of fire brings purity, gives you the character and foundation to be able to walk in the power and have sustained fruitfulness in your ministry and to be able to continue to lift up Jesus and keep the glory and the attention on Him. If there is impurity when the power starts flowing and you are not careful, you will start looking at yourself and at what God is doing through you and begin thinking God cannot do it through anybody else. Power not carried in the proper container can explode and blow things up creating a lot of damage.

The Fire Brings the Wind

So the forerunner brings a balanced message of power and purity. We need both. Fire is what burns away the dross. It burns away the chaff. In a recent quarterly prayer meeting with several pastors from the area we were discussing what the Spirit was saying to us and speaking to the church and what we were seeing God doing in this season in our region. One of the brothers shared that he was recently burning some rubbish. He started the fire because it was a good time to burn something as no wind was blowing. But once he started the fire, he noticed a breeze started blowing. He stated that this was a truth in the natural. When you light a fire and it burns up the oxygen in the atmosphere, a void, a vacuum is formed, it pulls the air. So in other words, the wind follows the fire. The fire brings the wind.

So He baptizes with the Holy Spirit and with fire. When God starts dealing with you about things in your life, laying the ax to the root, setting fire to things in your life that need to be burned out of you, it is going to bring the wind of the Spirit. It is interesting that on the day of Pentecost there were cloven tongues of fire and the sound of the wind came.

> But you shall receive power when the Holy Spirit has come upon you; and you shall be witnesses to Me in Jerusalem, and in all Judea and Samaria, and to the end of the earth."
> Act 1:8

Back in 1997, I became so desperate and disillusioned that I was ready to leave the ministry if I could not find more life in the Spirit than I was experiencing. My head was telling me one thing, and my heart was craving for another. God began showing me how empty I was. God started dealing with deficits in my life such as rejection and a performance mentality and a whole lot of pride. I started humbling myself, becoming broken, repenting, getting desperate, crying out and calling out to God. I realize now that God was baptizing me with fire. He was burning things out of me. It was not long after that, however, that the wind of the Holy Spirit started to blow. The fire will bring the wind. The fire has to do with purity and the wind has to do with power, the baptism of the spirit, the power.

The baptism of the Holy Spirit unleashes the power of God into your lives and ministry, but how do you know when you have it? Is it because you fall on the floor? Well, that happens sometimes. Is it because you speak in tongues? That happens sometimes. Is it because you shake uncontrollably? Well, that does happen sometimes. Do you feel the weightiness of God, and you become immobile in His presence? That happens sometimes. You burst out in laughter, and you cannot stop? Well, that happens sometimes. The

> Behold, I send the Promise of My Father upon you; but tarry in the city of Jerusalem until you are endued with power from on high.
> Luke 24:49

power has definitely come when you become a witness for Jesus Christ. You will have a boldness that you did not have before. You are ready to charge the hordes of Hell with a water pistol if God tells you.

When the Spirit came upon Saul, it turned him into a different man. When the Holy Spirit comes upon you and you receive the endument of power, according to Luke 24, you are filled with boldness and courageousness to become a witness with your life. Your life is

112

changed and your lips witness on demand. You witness with the power of the Spirit of God for people to be saved. You understand that we have to reach Jerusalem, Judea, and Samaria. We have to go to the uttermost parts of the Earth even if it means getting on a boat and driving down a river and visiting people who live in houses on top of stilts who have never heard about Jesus or never seen someone who looks like us before.

The baptism of the Spirit brings the power of God. It is not just so we can shake and have manifestations. It is what happens once you get up and get composed and hit the streets for Jesus that is the evidence of the enduement of power. Understand that these two baptisms, of fire and of the Spirit, are going to be working in your life. Forerunners need them in their lives and that is the message they will carry to others.

I used to argue with people that I had all the Holy Spirit that you can have and that I didn't need anything else, thank you very much. My wife argued with *me* after I got baptized with the Holy Spirit. She thought she had everything she needed. When she got up off the floor after being baptized in the Spirit, she was a different woman! She would go to the Christian bookstore and just lurk around, hoping somebody would come in with a limp so she could lay hands on them. I accused her of being a stalker. One night in a small and very informal service she interrupted the preacher, a friend of ours, while he was ministering to people after the sermon. She felt the Lord wanted her to pray for him! This was so out of the ordinary for her. She was changed by the enduement of power from on high. I still kid her telling her that she probably should have been locked up a few weeks till her feet touched earth once again.

> All of the sudden you might think, "Wow! I did not know there was so much God. I did not know it could be so good. I did not know that God still did this. I did not know that there was so much power!"

When the Spirit comes with power things are no longer the same. All of the sudden, your version of God expands and blows up. He becomes a great big God who can do great big things, and He can use little bitty you to do it!

The Dross and the Cross

He will baptize you with the Holy Spirit and with fire. The fire burns away the dross. When a silversmith heats up the metal and all the impurities, the dross, rise to the top. ^Q Then he scrapes off the dross leaving the pure silver. The baptism of fire burns away the impurities in your life, they rise to the top, and the Lord takes them away! The fire has to do with dross; the power has to do with the cross.

> **Fire and Dross**
> Fire is the most effectual means of purification. It is almost the only means by which the dross can be separated from the gold or silver. Scriptures frequently refer to it as an illustration of the process of the sanctification of the soul.

The Lord wants to get the dross out of your life so that the cross can begin to operate in your life. He uses the baptism of fire to burn out the dross, and it is the baptism of the Spirit that releases the power of the cross in your life. It is that same power that will enable you to crucify the flesh and its affections and walk in holiness carrying the message that God has given you to carry.

Practically speaking, the baptism of fire has to do with getting rid of what is not productive for God. John tells us the ax is laid to the root. Cut that tree down and do what? Throw it in the fire and burn it up, get rid of it, get it out of your life, and get it out of the way. The baptism of fire has a personal and practical application. It has to do with purifying your life. This can certainly be an uncomfortable experience that causes us to deal with issues we have swept away under the rug of forgetfulness, but nonetheless, God loves us too much to allow these dangers to lie dormant in the shadows of our souls.

Future Fire and Present Fire

There is also a prophetic message in the baptism of fire with an eschatological meaning. At the end of the age, Jesus will gather together those upon whom he has poured his Spirit, as His wheat into the barn.

---

^Q *If your life was heated up by a silversmith, what would rise to the top as dross?*

There will be an immersion of fire on everything else. Peter warned us of the fire of judgment. There is a fire for now, and there is a future fire that will take care of purging everything else.

There is an experience that is Biblical where the Holy Spirit of God comes upon the life of a believer and releases the *dunamis,* the power of God into that believer's life. Now, when you are saved, you are indwelt by the Holy Spirit. The indwelling ministry of the Holy Spirit happens at salvation. The "upon you" ministry of the Holy Spirit occurs when the Lord Jesus baptizes you, or immerses you into His power.

> **Dunamis (Greek)**
> Strength power, ability; inherent power, power residing in a thing by virtue of its nature, or which a person or thing exerts and puts forth; power for performing miracles.

It is an experience that is valid. It is vital, and it is vibrant in our lives. It is available to every believer. When that experience comes, sometimes there are manifestations. Sometimes you may fall into the floor. The presence of God comes upon you, the natural shuts down, and you cannot help it; you are just out. The Lord is doing spiritual surgery in your life. He is doing things inside of you.

Manifestation means that something is breaking out of the Spirit into the natural, and you can discern it with the physical senses. Sometimes it looks a little odd, a little peculiar, and a little different. However, all through the Scripture are references to different types of experiences happening to people when they are overcome by the glory of God.

I remember one time praying for a lady who had never been around the things of the Lord. I never even touched her. She just hit the floor and lay there for a while. When she came to, she was so frightened! We had to sit her down and explain through the Scriptures what had happened. She sensed the presence of God, but it was very frightening for her. She had never even heard the terminology and never seen it happen. But, it was very valid to her; the Holy Spirit just came upon her and met the hunger of her heart and fell upon her!

115

Before Jesus ever came onto the scene to begin his public ministry, isn't it interesting that God gave John a message to carry that included the baptism of the Holy Spirit? Even before Jesus was baptized in the water, before Jesus began his public ministry, John wanted to prepare the way of the Lord. One way you prepare for the Lord is to receive the baptism of the Holy Spirit and to let the baptism of fire do its work in your life. It is not something to shun; it is something to embrace because it is part of the forerunner anointing.

Jesus wants to do something for you man cannot do. Man can baptize you in water. Man can counsel you at the altar. Man can lay hands on you. However, if you get baptized in the Holy Spirit, and the Spirit begins to burn away the dross and chaff in your lives, it has to be the work of God. You have his promise that he wants to do it. He *will* baptize you with the Holy Spirit and with fire. Expect the fire of God to purify and to prepare you, and expect the Spirit of God to empower you.

When we stand before Him at the *Bema*, it is going to be a shameful thing there in the very presence of the Lord for him to have to burn that wood, hay, and stubble out of your life. You are going to realize then, that you had so many opportunities on Earth to allow Him to get unfruitful things out of your life so you could stand before Him in an honorable way. We need to be reminded that we will stand before Him, the Almighty God!

> **Bema** (Greek)
> Of the judgment seat of Christ. A raised platform in a synagogue from which the Pentateuch and the Prophets are read. In Grecian games athletes were awarded honor for victories at the bema. Paul used the term to connote the giving of rewards to church age believers.

A Personal Prayer

Father, I thank you. Thank you for the message of the baptism of the Spirit and the fire. Lord, thank you that you love me so much that you do not want me to live an unproductive, unfruitful life. You are willing to put your torch to the trash pile inside of me and burn it away so that what remains will be very productive. Thank you, Lord, that you can dredge the deep parts of my soul, and that you are willing to wade into the swampy, murky waters of my soul and dredge out those things that are hindering the flow of the Spirit. Thank you, Lord, that you are willing to take your flamethrower and burn way down deep into the recesses of my inner-person and burn out those things that are using up grace and energy and resources, but bearing no fruit.

Lord, I want to be faithful. I want to be fruitful. I want to be pure. I want to be powerful. I invite the ministry of your Holy Spirit. I want your Spirit to burn up the chaff. I want your Spirit to release more power inside of me. I want to be a pure vessel and a powerful vessel. I want to be able to carry the message for this season. I want to be a forerunner.

Holy Spirit, I do welcome you right now. I pray for your fire to burn, Lord, like it burned in the furnace the Hebrew children bound with ropes were thrown into. I pray that right now in the name of Jesus that ropes that have me bound would be burned — that I would be released from bondage, that I would be released from things that have shackled me, chained me and kept me away from you. I pray that you will put your torch to my wrong attitudes. Burn into me the fiery image of Jesus whose eyes are like coals of fire.

Lord, let your fire burn deep inside of me, making me more like your Son. Purge away the dross and the chaff, Lord. Let that fire start burning so it will bring the wind of God. I pray that the wind of God will be brought into the sails of my soul. Lord, I just pray that your Holy Spirit will come even now. I welcome you, Holy Spirit. In Jesus name, amen!

Chapter Fifteen

The Call for Fathers

After Malachi laid down his quill and the ink became dry on the papyrus script upon which he was writing, the last words to dry were the final words that would complete the Old Testament canon of Scripture. These words were on the heart of God knowing that there would be 400 years of prophetic silence that would follow. At the end of those 400 years, there would be a voice crying out in the wilderness to begin a new era of biblical history. Malachi ends his book with the revelation that a voice would come crying, and the New Testament begins with us hearing that voice.

> *... Says the Lord of hosts, "Remember the Law of Moses, My servant, which I commanded him in Horeb for all Israel, With the statutes and judgments. Behold, I will send you Elijah the prophet before the coming of the great and dreadful day of the Lord. And he will turn the hearts of the fathers to the children, and the hearts of the children to their fathers, Lest I come and strike the earth with a curse." Malachi 4: 3-6*

The Day of the Lord

When the phrase "the day of the Lord" occurs in the Bible, many times it carries with it several prophetic events some of which have already unfolded and some that will be unfolded. When you look at the terminology "the day of the Lord" in the Old Testament, you realize that it is a phrase encompassing several events. In Malachi, it encompasses the first and second coming of the Lord Jesus Christ. Peter preached from the book of Joel on the day of Pentecost and used the same passage to explain the outpouring of the Spirit that was taking place then as well as a series of cosmic events that will take place at the end of the age. Joel's prophecy does not denote this interval of time between the events of the first coming and the second coming but sees it all as an expression of the day of the Lord.

So, when Malachi writes about the dreadful and fearful day of the coming of the Lord, he is delivering a message from the Lord of judgment and wrath as well as the God of restoration and hope. And there is no inconsistency between these attributes of God. It is His passionate love that makes His fiery judgment necessary. He will always contend with everything that is inconsistent with love. This balance of heart is also in the message that a forerunner brings. The Lord promises to send us the "Spirit of Elijah" the prophet before the coming of the great and dreadful day of the Lord.

The Spirit that rested on John the Baptist prepared him to usher in the Lord's first coming. It will be the same Spirit that will rest on people prepared by the Lord prior to the second coming of Jesus. Remember, the forerunner is a person, or a people, prepared by the Lord. The Lord prepares them to prepare other people to prepare for the coming of the Lord. Jesus is preparing the preparers. So the forerunner carries message of preparation simply put "Get ready. The King is coming. When he shows up, be ready for Him."

The Turning of the Heart

In Malachi 4:6, we find that the spirit of the prophet will turn the hearts of fathers to their children and the hearts of the children to their fathers. The word *turn* is a repentance word. One thing God is telling us is that He is going to prepare a people, but first something has to happen in families. The hearts of the fathers have to be turned toward the children. The hearts of the children have to be turned toward the fathers.

The verse can also be a reference to the Abrahamic covenant, and how Israel has to turn back to what God had revealed to Abraham , the promise of the Messiah. That is part of the forerunner message. But it has to do, I believe, with even deeper issues. It has to do with what was in the

> **Abrahamic Covenant**
> God promised to bless the nations of the world through the nation of Israel (Genesis 12:1-3). The Abrahamic Covenant will be ultimately fulfilled upon the return of the Jesus to rescue and give blessing to Israel's people. One of the universal aspects of the covenant is blessings upon all the families of the earth through the Messiah.

heart of God when he created man, when he functioned as the first Father.

One characteristic of the forerunner anointing is that it results in the fathering spirit, or the fathering anointing. Let me tell you something, everyone, including me, needs fathering. All of us need fathering. It is so important.

Jealous Parents?

I do not know many parents who are jealous because their children have achieved more than they themselves did, are blessed more than they have been blessed, or are walking in deeper realms of the Spirit than they did. It is just natural for a parent's heart to rejoice that their children are venturing into territory they have not and enjoying favor and blessing beyond what they have known.

The heart of God is for His body to function like family. As long as there is jealousy and envy in the house, a family is not operating in the fathering anointing. Jacob showed favoritism towards Joseph, and it unleashed the opportunity for trouble under the roof. When a father walks in the love of God and fathers the way God wants him to, then much of the competition and jealousy is eliminated. This is true of our natural family structure but also of our spiritual family structure. We need spiritual fathers and mothers in our lives. God wants us to have spiritual fathers and spiritual mothers who we can look up to, and who because of their godly life, have the liberty to speak into our lives.

Paul talks about fathers compared to instructors in First Corinthians. An instructor is just somebody to tell you what to do. But the father is somebody who can impart to you what you need to be able to do what you need to do. In a home when a baby is born, you nurture, you train, you mentor and you get the child to the point where they can carry the family name and go out on their own.

> For though you might have ten thousand instructors in Christ, yet you do not have many fathers.
> 1 Corinthians 4: 15

As they ask for wisdom, you give them guidance, you continue to pray for them, and watch over them. That pattern came right out of the Bible.

120

The Lord wants His people to operate that way, striking a deathblow to competition, envy and jealousy. The spirit of Elijah turns the hearts of the fathers to the children, and the hearts of the children to the fathers.

Conflict over Inheritance

Too many spiritual sons want to remove their spiritual fathers and take their inheritance before the time, and too many spiritual fathers are withholding from their spiritual sons the inheritance that is theirs when it is time. So the giving and receiving becomes a war of pushing and pulling. This happens when there is not a true sense of family in the household of faith. When we operate by the patterns of the world, we get the results of the world. Corporate takeovers, power struggles, and managerial fallout become common because the "father-son" and "mother-daughter" relationships are too uncommon. A family increases its joy by accepting new faces into its circle. Without this heart, people become threatened when God begins raising someone up who has gifts that excel or differ from what the house has known.

I remember watching as a little boy in the early 1960s, the program which was very popular on television called "Father Knows Best". It was a weekly television program, featuring a nuclear family that propagated good moral values over the airwaves. It showed how parents solved problems and helped their children. Now, we are a couple of generations removed from that, and things have drastically changed for the average television family. Respect has been replaced by trash talk and manners have been eaten up by rudeness and vulgarity. This attitude tends to travel the airwaves right into the hearts and minds of our American families, and then we scratch our heads wondering what has happened. I don't mean to be cynical, but the effect of moral erosion is robbing the household of faith of the honor and respect it needs to see the favor of God on its families.

I remind you that Malachi prophesized that, "The hearts of the fathers must be turned to the children and the hearts of the children must be turned to the fathers, lest I come and strike the Earth with a curse." We can conclude that if this fathering anointing is not present in

121

a congregation, community, or society, the curse begins to spread. Anger, violence, poverty, and illegitimacy are all signs of a curse on the broken family structure. When we get out from under the Father's covering, we get out from under the Father's favor. When Adam and Eve got out from under the covering of the Father, they got out from under the Father's favor. There is a blessing of God on family as God intended it to be.

The Tragic Toll of Fatherlessness

Statistics inform us that ninety percent of all homeless and runaway children are from fatherless homes. Eighty-five percent of all children who exhibit behavioral disorders come from fatherless homes. Eighty percent of rapists motivated with displaced anger come from fatherless homes. Seventy-one percent of all high school dropouts come from fatherless homes. Seventy-five percent of all adolescent patients in chemical abuse centers come from fatherless homes. Seventy percent of juveniles in state-operated institutions come from fatherless homes. Eighty-five percent of all youths sitting in prisons grew up in a fatherless home.

When you interpret all this, it means that children from a fatherless home situation are five times more likely to commit suicide, thirty-two times more likely to run away, twenty times more likely to have behavioral disorders, fourteen times more likely to commit rape, nine times more likely to drop out of high school, ten times more likely to abuse chemical substances, nine times more likely to end up in a state operated institution, and twenty times more likely to end up in prison.

Studies show that children who lose a parent during their childhood, not just through death, but by any means, are much more likely to be prone to major depression, to have bipolar disorder and to have schizophrenia. One survey said that half of Americans agree that most people have unresolved problems with their fathers. There are an estimated twenty-five million children, or 36.6 percent of the children in our country who do not have a father in the home. In the post-war generation, eighty percent of children grew up with two biological parents who were married to each other. Today, only about fifty percent of children will spend their entire childhood in an intact family. What these statistics indicate is that a child who does not have a father at home has a lot more obstacles to overcome in order to be successful and enjoy life as God intended it to be enjoyed.

God is Father to the Fatherless

I want to encourage those of you in single-parent households that our God promises to be a father to the fatherless. Your Heavenly Father says He will be a father to the fatherless. God takes it very personally when a child does not have a daddy. It is so important for single mothers or single fathers to tell their child the Heavenly Father will be there for them and bridge the gap for them. If you do not do that, and they do not learn to depend on their Heavenly Father for covering, then trouble is coming. Even secular society recognizes it.

Satan always moves to uncover and expose. When God created Adam and Eve, He was a covering for them, and Adam became covering for Eve. It is the glory of the Lord to conceal a matter. God wants us to have His covering. That is the reason why God promises to be a covering for a child that is fatherless. So it is easy to understand that the enemy has laid out a clever, methodical plan to strike the home at its heart. The enemy realizes that before the return of Christ, the spirit of Elijah is going to be poured out, and that spirit is going to cause the fathers and children to start reconciling, ministering together, and walking together in agreement. He realizes that God is going to work to bring the generations together and that a trans-generational anointing is poured out through the spirit of Elijah. Bridges will be built instead of burned, and homes will warm up under the fire of revival between parents and their children. How glorious to see the generational gap replaced by extended arms of love!

> Sing praises to God and to his name! Sing loud praises to him who rides the clouds. His name is the Lord – rejoice in his presence! Father to the fatherless, defender of widows – this is God, whose dwelling is holy.
> Psalm 68:4-5

Satan's Strategy Against the Home

You can understand how the enemy would want to strike the family by pushing dad out of the home, then pushing mom out of the home, and then striking the womb of America. The enemy figures that if God is going to raise up a

> *And the Lord God formed man of the dust of the ground, and breathed into his nostrils the breath of life; and man became a living being. Genesis 2:7*

generation to carry this forerunner anointing, then he'll just take them out before they get a chance to even get started! Legalized abortion is part of the strategy of Satan to stifle and stop the voice of the prophetic generation that God wants to raise up. God is moving to turn hearts towards fathers, and Satan is standing against it.

Secular researchers have studied our abusive culture, and they have determined a core issue. They have coined a new phrase to express what the problem is. The new phrase that has been coined is called *Father Hunger*. Research has indicated that one of the core issues in our society that is causing things to head the wrong way is Father Hunger; dad is not home.[Q] However, dads can be at home, and still be absentee. Dads can check out emotionally and check out spiritually. Thankfully, God is beginning to work in the hearts of those of us who are fathers and those of us who have the fathering anointing. When this anointing begins to move with power, you find yourself desiring to cover, protect, provide and impart into the lives of your children.

There are natural fathers. There are spiritual fathers. There is our Heavenly Father. You may have a deficit when it comes to a natural father for whatever reasons,and you may have been so abused,

> *Therefore a man shall leave his father and mother and be joined to his wife, and they shall become one flesh. Genesis 2:24*

mistreated and hurt that you reject men all together, but you can still have spiritual fathering in your life. Your Heavenly Father will still be Father of your life. God will make sure of that if you will let your

---

[Q] *Do you know of someone who might have father hunger? What could you do to help satisfy their father hunger?*

124

heart be turned toward fathers. Our hearts yearn for Father's love.

He's Daddy God!

The first occurrence of the word Father in the Old Testament is in Genesis 2: 24. Adam was formed out of the dust of the ground. God breathed His breath into Adam. The first face that Adam saw was God's. The first voice that Adam heard was God's. The first conscious awareness that Adam ever had was of the presence of God. These firsts are important; so is this first occurrence of the word Father.

Imagine God hovering over a lump of dirt that is Adam. Just imagine God hovering. God breathes His breath into that lump of dirt that is to become Adam. Now, I want you to do something for me. I want you to open your mouth wide. Now take in a slow deep breath and hold it for a second. Did you hear that sound? *A-w-w-w-b-b-b.* Do it again. *A-w-w-w-b-b-b.* That is the sound of the Hebrew word for Father. Transliterated, it is spelled *awb.* Alphabetically, it is also the first word in the Hebrew Lexicon. That is what it sounds like. *A-w-w-w-b-b-b.* God breathes on Adam. Adam's Father breathes on him. He awakens, sees the face of his Father, his lungs are filled with the breath of God, and as he receives it, he the sound of "Father" fills his lungs. I believe when Adam received life with the sound *awb,* he was saying, "Father." We were made to live in the way that God is our *awb,* our Father. The first word out of Adam's mouth was "Daddy."

> *Pure religion and undefiled before God and the Father is this, to visit the fatherless and widows in their affliction, and to keep himself unspotted from the world.*
> James 1:27

> **Abba** (Semitic)
> Father; used in prayer and communion with God.

> **Orphanos** (Greek)
> Fatherless; bereft of a father, of parents.

Jesus came as God in the flesh, and He demonstrated to His disciples how to live under the covering of the Father when He said, "I do not do anything except what I see Father doing. What I speak is what I hear the Father speaking." The life of the Father was in Christ, and He mentored his disciples. The night before the crucifixion, He gathered them together and assured them that he would not leave them as orphans. We are told in James 1:27 about the importance of caring for the orphans.

A father comforts, encourages, and strengthens. Dads in the home ought to be like the Holy Spirit, and we ought to minister like the Holy Spirit ministers to us. We ought to minister to our children through the power of the Holy Spirit. Jesus did not leave us fatherless. When he ascended, he poured out the gift of the Father. He poured out the gift of the Holy Spirit. Paul assures us in Romans 8:15 that the gift of the Holy Spirit is given to allow us to cry out Abba, which means papa or daddy. Dear reader, we will not know the depths of joy, peace, contentment, and liberty until we have a right relationship with Abba, our Father.

The wrinkles, spots and blemishes that are in Christ's bride must be removed, and His bride must be cleansed and purified before his return. The hearts of the fathers must be turned towards the children, and the hearts of the children must be turned towards the father before his return. This change of hearts will do away with the generation gap and the separation between older and younger members of congregations. God does not want separation between ages in His church.

When fathers get their hearts right toward their children, they encourage, comfort, instruct, impart, and correct them. Fathers want to raise them to a point, and then release them so they can go further than they themselves have ever gone! If we are going to go on for God as sons and daughters, we cannot have arrogance, pride and wrong attitudes about the older or the younger generation. We have to honor those who have gone before us because they were forerunners, and we must trust in the younger generation and in God who will raise them up to serve Him in new and powerful capacities.

When you have a family attitude about the people of God, you want to take care of your kids and honor your parents. But when we let pride in and have the western culture's individualistic and independent attitudes, then that creates all kinds of problems.

Bringing the Generations Together

When I was first filled with the Spirit and my life went through such a change, I went through a season in which I felt very isolated and alone. The Baptists thought I was too Pentecostal and involved with Holy Spirit experiences. Then, the people who were open and flowing in the Spirit were skeptical of me because of my Baptist background. So, I was hungry for somebody to teach me and answer my hundreds of questions. Things were going on that I did not understand. I wanted somebody tell me what was happening. I was having experiences I did not know you could have. I wanted somebody to help me.

The Lord started sending people to help me. Thank God, Pastor Henry Melton opened his arms and loved me from day one, and gave me an opportunity to express the gift that the Lord had put on my life. There were a few others the Lord would raise up. Bill French in Birmingham, Alabama, helped me tremendously. I could go visit him and ask him question, and he mentored me. The Lord sends people because we need them! We were made to have a father or mother watching over us and speaking into our life. There is protection and security when you have the right covering.[Q]

But sin comes and turns the heart

> He administers justice for the fatherless and the widow, and loves the stranger, giving him food and clothing. Therefore love the stranger, for you were strangers in the land of Egypt.
> Deuteronomy 10:18-19
>
> You shall not pervert justice due the stranger or the fatherless, nor take a widow's garment as a pledge.
> Deuteronomy 24:17
>
> When you reap your harvest in your field, and forget a sheaf in the field, you shall not go back to get it; it shall be for the stranger, the fatherless, and the widow, that the LORD your God may bless you in all the work of your hands.
> Deuteronomy 24:19

[Q] Who acts as a spiritual father or mother in your life? How long has it been since you have poured your heart out to them?

127

of the father away from the child. The child gets rebellious or the child goes away from the father because the father causes them to feel rejected. Many people are carrying a lot of rejection issues. God does not want you to feel that way. He loves you. He accepts you. He wants you to embrace His love, but you have to allow fear to be moved aside by God's love. You have to have humility and be willing to receive instruction and correction.

> The helpless commits himself to You; You are the helper of the fatherless.
> Psalm 10:14
>
> To do justice to the fatherless and the oppressed, that the man of the earth may oppress no more.
> Psalm 10: 18
>
> A father of the fatherless, a defender of widows, Is God in His holy habitation.
> Psalm 68:5

Recently, someone who is a spiritual father to me spoke correction into my life. It hurt, but it hurt good. I needed it. God used the correction to make me more like Christ. God will use correction in your life to help you become more Christ-like. Forerunner preparatory school will involve correction. Part of the forerunner anointing is this fathering characteristic.

Lost Coverings

God takes the fatherless issue and the need for the fathering anointing seriously. Verses from Deuteronomy tell us about His instructions to His people under the Old Covenant. The widow and the fatherless, who do they represent? They represent a person whose covering is gone, a wife whose husband dies and a child who does not have a father. They are those who have no one to provide covering and protection and security and provision. Therefore, God tells us to help make up a covering in the life of these people who have lost their covering. We are to love them and care for them, and give them the covering they do not have. Do you want to be blessed? Be involved in giving to the fatherless and helping the widows.

David describes God's own fatherly heart in the Psalms. David, himself, certainly learned the lessons of being fathered and comforted by his Heavenly Father as he ran and hid from Saul who could have been a mentor in his life but instead sought to end his life. Later, David would feel the sting of being rejected by one of his own son's, Absalom, who attempted to remove him from the throne so that he could take his place.

> *I do not write these things to shame you, but as my beloved children I warn you.... in Christ Jesus I have begotten you through the gospel. Therefore I urge you, imitate me. For this reason I have sent Timothy to you, who is my beloved and faithful son in the Lord...*
> 1 Corinthians 4: 14-17

All of us need fathering. Part of the result of the forerunner anointing being operative in the body of Christ is the raising up of spiritual fathers and mothers. Spiritual fathers and mothers are being raised up to parent spiritual children and to get them to the point where *they* are released to become fathers and mothers.

Jesus constantly reminded his followers about his Heavenly Father. He taught us to pray, "Our Father, which art in Heaven." He told us that our Heavenly Father, "Would forgive us as we forgive others." Sometimes people carry rejection and bitterness because of what their earthly Dad did, and sometimes it is because of what he did not do. I guarantee you the devil wants you to continue to harbor bitterness. Let me tell you something, unforgiveness and bitterness in your heart toward your earthly father will keep the Heavenly Father's forgiveness from being appropriated in your life. In other words, you are going to be in bondage until you are willing to forgive your earthly father for what he may have done to you or may not have done for you. After you forgive, you move on and operate with God as your Heavenly Father. Jesus taught us to see God as our Heavenly Father.

People are Looking for Fathers

Receiving His love enables us to start walking in this fathering anointing. Paul spiritually fathered many sons such as Timothy and Titus. He sacrificed to pour himself into them. If you are going to be father or mother to other people by operating with the forerunner fathering anointing, what has to happen first? You have to be healed so you can respond to God as your Heavenly Father, your Daddy God. He is going to heal your heart so that you can walk in that dimension of love that has been modeled to you and demonstrated in you so that you can impart to others and begin to father or mother them. I encourage you to be spiritually mature and to be sensitive to others who want to receive from you. That is usually how you know if the Lord wants you to be a spiritual father or mother. You begin seeing hungry people wanting to spend time with you. You start speaking into their lives.

All of us need fathering and mothering in our lives. Paul talked about nursing the baby Christians at Thessalonica like a mother does her child. In First Corinthians 4, he referred to Timothy as his son in the faith and to himself as being a father to the church at Corinth.

Paul wrote to the Corinthians with a warning and urged them to imitate his own behavior. That is part of being a father. You can tell your children to get straightened out before you get there, and then we can have a good time. Then you tell them that if they don't get straightened out, that when you get there you are going to straighten them out, and *then* we will have a good time. This is what Paul basically told the church at Corinth. Why could he do that? He could do that because he had a relationship with the church.

> *What do you want? Shall I come to you with a rod, or in love and a spirit of gentleness?*
> 1 Corinthians 4:21

> *But we were gentle among you, just as a nursing mother cherishes her own children.*
> *...as you know how we exhorted, and comforted, and charged every one of you, as a father does his own children, that you would walk worthy of God who calls you into His own kingdom and glory.*
> 1 Thessalonians 2:7, 11

If somebody is going to speak correction in your life, they should have a loving relationship with you. I do not like it too much when lone rangers come up and want to correct me. These people who have no relationship with me and do not have any idea what is going on in my life just presume that can start correcting. I am not saying that God can't speak through someone like this. However, it would be the exception rather than the rule. The Bible says to know (have relationship with) those who labor among you. Be careful whom you let father and mother you, because if they are not healed, they cannot lead you into wholeness.

Do you understand that we all need fathering and mothering? If you are going to grow and mature in the Lord, you need to be under the covering of someone who is more spiritually mature than you and who loves you. Then you can be trained, learn submission, and grow. None of us are exempt from that, and the desire for covering is part of this forerunner anointing that God is beginning to release. The forerunner anointing may also cause your heart to be drawn to others to speak into their lives and impart into their lives. You feel your heart being drawn to that person to become a spiritual father or mother to them. If it is the Lord, they will usually come to you or want to hang out around you and ask questions. They will pursue you like a child does his/her daddy or mother.

A natural father, a spiritual father, a Heavenly Father – our heart has to be turned and made whole in all three areas. If your have or had a natural father and things are not right in your relationship with him, you can get things right in your heart now. Maybe you have tried every way you know to make things right, but your efforts were not received. Well, just keep praying, loving, and keep your door open, and keep working on your relationship with your Heavenly Father.

You may have been so hurt in churches in days gone by that you can hardly trust somebody to spiritually father you or spiritually mother you. You are afraid you are going to get betrayed. You are afraid you are going to get stung. You are afraid you are going to get hurt. So what do you do? You just keep that old wall of rejection up and you come and sit in the pew and have a pretty good time but you know deep inside, you are hungry. You are hungry for somebody to look you in the eye and speak into your life.

Get healed so that you can move on with God, the Heavenly Father. What view of Him do you have now? You know how your life started. That is where you need to be now – receiving His breath. *Abba! You are my life! Everything I need comes from you. You are the source; you are the origin. In you, I live and move and have my breathing and my being. It is*

131

your breath, Lord that fills my lungs. When He becomes your life, then you can start receiving from others, growing and correctly relating in the natural realm.

The forerunner prepares people to be preparers of people. So the first step to receiving the forerunner anointing is letting God heal you so that you can be prepared to help someone else find healing. Some people need more healing than others. You may have been treated by your earthly father in ways that a child should never be treated. You need to know that God's heart is broken for you, but God did not do that to you. He was there, and that is the reason you made it. That is the reason you survived. That is the reason you are alive today. He wants to love you in a way that your heart has always hungered for.

Men and women are faulty. None of us are perfect, but there are people that will love you. Get healed so that God can use you as a forerunner to turn the hearts of the fathers to the children and the hearts of the children to the fathers. I want to encourage you to do what Adam did in his first moment of life. He received the breath of God, and that is what you need to do today. You need to receive what the Lord wants to impart in your life. You need to receive the healing from the heart of the Father.

It may be that God will begin speaking to you about taking some steps of reconciliation. If you slammed the door on your relationship with your earthly father, it needs to be opened. You may not know what is keeping you from having a loving relationship with your earthly father. But the Heavenly Father knows, and He knows that thing is keeping you from being able to receive from Him what He wants to give you. We were all made for that, and that is where we are all heading. Just let Him do it now.

A Personal Prayer

Father God, Abba, I thank you for giving me the breath of life and for allowing me to live in this season. Lord, I thank you that you are releasing the forerunner anointing even today, reminding me of your grace and mercy that you give to those who are willing to be changed. Lord, I pray that you will make me whole and that your love will move with such power in my life that any hate, rejection, or anger that fills me with fear will be washed away as I repent of any wrong attitude I have toward my natural or spiritual father or mother, or even towards you, Heavenly Father. Lord, I pray that as I learn to grow in your Fatherly love that I will grow in maturity of spirit.

I call out to you, Abba! I want all that you have for me! Heal my heart! Turn my heart towards you! Turn my heart towards my children. Turn my heart towards my natural father. Turn my heart towards my stepfather. Change and position my heart as you want it so I can receive what you want to give me and be who you want me to be. Father God, breathe on me and help me to receive your love into the depth of my innermost being. Lor,d I pray that I would begin to walk in greater depths of your love and that I will look to you as my Heavenly Father. I ask for your Father's blessing to be poured out on me. The Spirit in me cries out"Abba!" I love you! I thank you, Lord, that you know my name, and I bless your name. In Jesus name, amen!

Web Sources Used for Fatherless Statistics

http://www.fathersforlife.org/divorce/chldrndiv.htm
http://www.mensrights.com.au/page17g.htm
http://fathersloveletter.com/Ministry/statistics.html

Chapter Sixteen

The Forerunner and Jezebel

Beyond the boundaries of what can be seen with the natural eye, there are at work demonic forces aimed at the forerunner messenger. Among those demonic forces in the unseen realm, is the spirit that worked through the ancient Jezebel who so hated Elijah the prophet. When at Jehu's orders the eunuchs cast Jezebel down off the wall and the dogs licked the blood that oozed from her dead body, the spirit(s) that worked so wickedly through her simply went in search of another host. It may be that somewhere along the path you are forerunning, you may find yourself in a standoff with someone who is listening to the deceptive voice of the spirit that spoke through Jezebel.

There is still a correlation between the ministry of the forerunner, the spirit of Elijah, and the operation of the spirit of Jezebel. Part and parcel of the release of the forerunner anointing has to do with the addressing and pulling down of the powers of the spirit of Jezebel.

It is important to understand that when I use the term Jezebel I am talking about a spirit, not a person. Now the spirit can manifest through a person, but when we talk about Jezebel, we are talking about the operation of a spirit against a person, against a people, against a move of God, or against a congregation. The name Jezebel has its roots in the Old Testament story of Ahab, the King of Israel, and his wicked wife Jezebel. Elijah was confronted by Jezebel herself, by the prophets of Jezebel and, behind the scenes, the spirit that worked through

Groves
Probably collections of wooden pillars that were idols of the Canaanite goddess of the sea, Asherah.

Ashtoreth
Consort of Baal. Queen of Heaven. Women made sacramental cakes to honor her.

⁹Now therefore, send and gather all Israel to me on Mount Carmel, the four hundred and fifty prophets of Baal, and the four hundred prophets of Asherah, who eat at Jezebel's table."
1 Kings 18:19

Jezebel.

The spirit of Elijah is being poured out in our day, just as the spirit of Elijah was poured out on John the Baptist, the forerunner, to prepare the way for the first coming of Christ. The spirit of Elijah is being poured out on forerunners now to prepare people for the Second Coming of Christ. As Elijah operated in the Old Testament to bring restoration to the nation of Israel and to tear down the idolatry of the worship of Baal, Ashtoreth, and the Groves, he was confronted by the spirit that worked through Jezebel. Today, we might as well expect that a forerunner operating under the spirit of Elijah will also be confronted by the spirits that knew Jezebel's bidding.

Hell Standing Against Heaven

Jezebel herself had 450 prophets of Baal, and 400 prophets of the Groves. They all did the bidding of this wicked queen. I am rather certain that Lucifer's lips stayed close to Jezebel's ear. He whispered his maniacal, demonic plans into her hearing, and then she would voice what she heard, almost prophetically. We see that the spirit of Jezebel does operate through the prophetic in the book of the Revelation. Satan works through the person with the spirit of Jezebel to release his decrees to stand against what God desires to do. However, it is the spirit of Elijah that releases the prophetic spirit to voice the decrees and declare the will of God in the Earth, to usher in restoration, and to prepare people for the coming of the Lord.

It is the old story of Hell standing against Heaven; Satan standing against God; the false prophet standing against the true prophet; the spirit of Jezebel operating against the spirit of Elijah; the forerunner being confronted by the staller. The whole purpose of the spirit of Jezebel is to shut

> Now Ahab the son of Omri did evil in the sight of the Lord, more than all who were before him. And it came to pass ... that he took as wife Jezebel the daughter of Ethbaal, king of the Sidonians; and he went and served Baal and worshiped him. Then he set up an altar for Baal in the temple of Baal, which he had built in Samaria. And Ahab made a wooden image. Ahab did more to provoke the Lord God of Israel to anger than all the kings of Israel who were before him.
> 1 Kings 16:30-33

135

down the prophetic and the operation of God in the Earth. When God begins to produce a new wineskin to bring about a shift in His body on the Earth, He begins to release the prophetic. Remember, He does nothing except He reveals it to His prophets, then the prophet releases and decrees what has been revealed.

The Prophetic Element of Prayer

There is a prophetic element to prayer. When you pray the way Jesus taught you to pray, "Kingdom of God, come," you are speaking prophetically. You are decreeing in the realm of Earth what God has decreed in the courts of Heaven. We need to understand our position as intercessors as the Lord's people here on Earth. Prophetic prayer is part of the forerunner anointing, and the spirit of Jezebel will operate against it.

The word "Jezebel" occurs in the Bible 22 times. The vast majority of occasions are in the Old Testament, although her name is mentioned in the Book of Revelation. It is interesting that her name means 'Baal exalts'. Baal was a false god of the Old Testament. It means "Baal is husband to," or "unchaste." So, when you study these meanings, it is as if Jezebel means "my husband is Baal," or "I am married to Baal." The Scripture tells us that the prophets of Baal sat and ate at Jezebel's table. This spirit is always looking for a person who will serve as its host or hostess. Through Jezebel's authority these false prophets were allowed to be fattened from the coins of King Ahab's purse. Unfortunately, there are many in our day who are unwittingly supplying their hospitality to this spirit.

And Elijah the Tishbite, of the inhabitants of Gilead, said to Ahab, "As the Lord God of Israel lives, before whom I stand, there shall not be dew nor rain these years, except at my word."

When you study Jezebel in the Old Testament, you realize she was a very committed Baal-worshiper. Her father was a Baal-worshiper, a pagan king, and Ahab, king of Israel, took her as his wife. When he married Jezebel, she brought witchcraft into Israel's palace. The Bible tells us how wicked Ahab was. Then, God had enough!

136

Decreeing the Will of Heaven

All of a sudden, Elijah the Tishbite appears on the scene, out of nowhere, there he is, *the Prophet of God!* He stands before the king and begins to decree the will of Heaven. Elijah goes before Ahab, and he decrees that because Ahab is doing wicked and evil in the sight of the Lord, worshiping Baal, and bringing idolatry into the land, that there will not be rain, except by his word. Now, Elijah was using authority! That is learning how to hear from God and being confident that you have heard from God! That is an understanding of your authority. Three years later, it had still not rained.

> And Ahab told Jezebel all that Elijah had done, also how he had executed all the prophets with the sword. Then Jezebel sent a messenger to Elijah, saying, "So let the gods do to me, and more also, if I do not make your life as the life of one of them by tomorrow about this time."
> 1 Kings 19:1-2

Ahab tried to kill the man who had the authority to make it rain, even knowing that without rain, they would all die. This shows you how demonic Jezebel was; she threatened to kill off what her nation most needed. Across this land what is most needed is a genuine, authentic, spiritual awakening in the church. This would bring an awakening across this nation moving it to repentance, turning toward Jesus Christ as Lord of Lord, and King of Kings.

> "Hear me, O Lord, hear me, that this people may know that You are the Lord God, and that You have turned their hearts back to You again." Then the fire of the Lord fell and consumed the burnt sacrifice, and the wood and the stones and the dust, and it licked up the water that was in the trench.
> And Elijah said to them, "Seize the prophets of Baal! Do not let one of them escape!" So they seized them; and Elijah brought them down to the Brook Kishon and executed them there.
> 1 Kings 18:37-38, 40

One of the spirits that stands against this happening is the spirit of Jezebel. The spirit of Jezebel can operate in your marriage. The spirit of Jezebel can operate in your work place. The spirit of Jezebel can operate in your home and your family. The spirit of Jezebel can operate in the classroom. One of the favorite places for Jezebel to do her bidding is in the church of the Lord Jesus Christ

> Then the Lord said to him: "Go, return on your way to the Wilderness of Damascus; and when you arrive, anoint Hazael as king over Syria. Also you shall anoint Jehu the son of Nimshi as king over Israel. And Elisha the son of Shaphat of Abel Meholah you shall anoint as prophet in your place.
> 1 Kings 19:15-16

because it is most likely that is where the prophetic voice is going to begin to arise. The spirit of Jezebel operates to suffocate, stifle, and stop the prophetic voice of God's people. The silencing of the prophetic voice is objective number one. Once the true prophetic voice is silenced, the false can have its way.

Schemes that Silence

You can study the operation of the spirit of Jezebel through the scripture. Elijah was the prophet, he was the spokesperson of God. He was carrying the message of God on his lips, and Jezebel wanted to kill him! John the Baptist came on the scene in the New Testament carrying the message of God on his lips to bring about repentance. He came to change and prepare the people for the first coming of the Lord. Ultimately, Herodias, a woman, whom I believe was also under the operation of the spirit of Jezebel, so hated him that she had him beheaded. She would not be happy until she had in her hands the head that housed the mouth that released the prophetic words of the Lord.

Now that is an example of what Jezebel wants to do in your life when you begin standing up and decreeing the will of God in your marriage, in the life of your children, in the workplace, in the classroom, in the church, in the community, and in the government. It is the spirit of Jezebel that stands against and is working through human civil government to shut down any mention of God, certainly any mention of Jesus and even any posting of the Ten Commandments. It wants to remove the name of God in our pledge and off our money! What is behind this? It is the spirit of Jezebel that wants to shut down any mention or acknowledgement of the true God. When it becomes illegal to mention the true God, the way is made for the proliferation of Jezebel's schemes that diverts worship to the "Baal" of her choosing.

It is interesting how God works. Elijah went to Mount Carmel and called fire down from Heaven, and ultimately the prophets of Baal and the prophets of the Grove were slain. Remember that, 850 altogether? Jezebel's messengers were silenced. And, remember, Jezebel threatened to kill Elijah! She was after him, and he ran. He got discouraged, and was ready to die. God ministered to him and reminded him that there were 7,000 people who had not yet bowed to Baal. Then He gave him some things to do. He told Elijah to anoint Hazael king of Syria.

The Governmental Mantle

In other words, go to a pagan land and anoint a person and put a king in place! Do you know that God, even in countries that do not acknowledge Him, is moving in this Earth to put people in position to bring about revolution and change in those countries? He does that today. I believe that is what happened in Uganda, a whole nation that has now turned to Christ. The heart of the king is in the hand of the Lord, and He turns it like rivers of water where ever He wills.

> And Elisha the prophet called one of the sons of the prophets, and said to him, "Get yourself ready, take this flask of oil in your hand, and go to Ramoth Gilead. Now when you arrive at that place, look there for Jehu the son of Jehoshaphat, the son of Nimshi, and go in and make him rise up from among his associates, and take him to an inner room. Then take the flask of oil, and pour it on his head, and say, 'Thus says the Lord: "I have anointed you king over Israel."
> 2 Kings 9:1-3

God began giving Elijah things to do, and it is interesting how God began to use the person carrying the prophetic mantle, Elisha, to release anointing to those who would walk under the kingly mantle. It is interesting that He anointed Jehu, as written in 2 Kings 9. It is important for you to understand this scripture so you understand the weight of governmental authority in the heavenlies.

It is the mantle of government that the spirit of Jezebel attacks and works through to stop the prophetic. It is the king or the person carrying the governmental authority in a structure that becomes the weapon of the spirit of Jezebel. In a church, the spirit could work through a pastor or an individual who can influence enough people in a church to cause division and disloyalty toward God's leadership. If you think about it, Jezebel was the power behind the throne of Ahab. Ahab was king, but what did Ahab do? He did what Jezebel told him. Jezebel worked through the king, and Ahab began issuing the decrees to kill the prophet Elijah.

When John the Baptist came on the scene in the New Testament, we are told that he operated in the spirit of Elijah. The Gospel of Mark, Chapter 6, tells us the story of John's death. King Herod's wife, Herodias, wanted John dead much earlier. She hated him, but the Bible says Herod feared John because he knew he was a holy and devout man. Herod would not touch John. He put John in prison because he did not like what John was preaching to him. John told him that he was not supposed to be with his brother's wife. But he would go and hear John, and there was almost a love-hate relationship that Herod had with John. He loves him, but he hates him; he hates him, but he loves him. Herod would not kill John.

> So the young man, the servant of the prophet, went to Ramoth Gilead. And when he arrived, there were the captains of the army sitting; and he said, "I have a message for you, Commander." Jehu said, "For which one of us?" And he said, "For you, Commander." Then he arose and went into the house. And he poured the oil on his head, and said to him, "Thus says the LORD God of Israel: 'I have anointed you king over the people of the LORD, over Israel. You shall strike down the house of Ahab your master, that I may avenge the blood of My servants the prophets, and the blood of all the servants of the LORD, at the hand of Jezebel. For the whole house of Ahab shall perish; and I will cut off from Ahab all the males in Israel, both bond and free. So I will make the house of Ahab like the house of Jeroboam the son of Nebat, and like the house of Baasha the son of Ahijah
> 2 Kings 9:4-9

Promises Made Under Perverted Pressure

Then, Herodias sent her daughter Salomé to dance for Herod, and Herod's hormones started boiling. She got him all stirred up. Then, what does he start doing? He starts decreeing with kingly authority that Salomé can have just about anything she wanted from him. Now, just think, Salomé could have had half the kingdom. Think of the money, the riches, the land, the houses that could have been hers. But her mother told her to ask for the head of John the Baptist on a platter. Hate is a powerful thing. Her hate for the Prophet was greater than her greed for riches. She wanted blood not bounty!

What caused Herod the king to say, "Wow, woman, I will give you whatever you want."? Was it not through sexual enticement?

Herod had made an oath that Salomé could have what ever she wanted. He immediately issued an execution order and John's head was severed from his shoulders and brought to Herodias on a platter. Who issued the decree for John's head to fall? Herod the king issued the decree. The spirit of Jezebel operated through Herodias and Salomé to stir up the heart of the king. In 2 Kings Nine, the spirit of Elijah is being confronted by Jezebel. God told Elijah to anoint Jehu to be king over Israel. It is interesting! Guess whom God used to take down Jezebel? The same authority that she worked through was the same authority that God used to cast her down. This shows the level of authority that is upon the king. I want to remind you that you are part of a kingdom of priests and kings. The working of the spirit of Jezebel does confront civil human government, but it also confronts apostolic government in the Kingdom. It is the prophetic voice that Jezebel wants to silence, but it is apostolic authority that God often works through to silence her voice. The story of apostolic authority is told in Second Kings Nine through the account of the anointing of Jehu as king. At that time, Jehu was commander of the army, and the servants of the Lord and the prophets of the Lord had been killed by Jezebel. Ahab, his

> And when Herodias' daughter herself came in and danced, and pleased Herod and those who sat with him, the king said to the girl, "Ask me whatever you want, and I will give it to you." He also swore to her, "Whatever you ask me, I will give you, up to half my kingdom. So she went out and said to her mother, "What shall I ask?" And she said, "The head of John the Baptist!" Immediately she came in with haste to the king and asked, saying, "I want you to give me at once the head of John the Baptist on a platter."
> Mark 6:22-25

141

dad, his dad's dad, and his dad's dad's dad were wicked. It was a wicked family line, and God had had enough, so He stopped the family line. There was a paradigm shift and a radical change in the kingdom. God anointed someone else to be king.

So, the prophet Elisha heard the word of the Lord, received the word of the Lord, released the word of the Lord, and anointed and established the king. The king then carried the mantle of king and walked in governmental authority, given to him by God, to cast down Jezebel. The very position that Jehu then occupied is the very position that Jezebel had been working through to lead Israel in idolatry.

Praying for the Shift

In a nation God will move and work to take out kings and put in kings, to take out presidents and put in presidents, who will decree His will. God will work to bring about a shift, an alignment, and a change so that He can begin to release what He wants to release to bring about His purposes in the Earth. But the warfare is in the Heavenlies, and so we must pray. Our prayers play into these shiftings that must occur in order to stop Jezebel's dominion.

I believe that blessed are the people whose God is the Lord. Righteousness exalts a nation, but sin is a reproach to many people. Treasures of wickedness profit nothing. So, it is not about economic strategy; it is about righteousness. When you birth righteousness, blessing is going to follow, it is called the favor of God.

We need to understand that our prayers are powerfully important in this issue. Every forerunner must be committed to and have an established life of prayer where he/she spends much time soaking in the presence of the true King. Jehu was anointed king over Israel to bring an end to the rule and reign of Jezebel. God used governmental authority to bring that about. Jezebel worked through the established authority to silence the prophetic voice. She worked through Ahab to try to stop Elijah. The spirit of Jezebel worked through Herod to cut the head off of John the Baptist, and the spirit of Jezebel works today against those who would be proclaimers, especially prophetic proclaimers of what God wants to release in this Earth.

The spirit of Jezebel works through governmental authority both civilly and spiritually. Some nations have passed laws making it illegal to preach in the church against homosexuality. Laws that state you cannot say homosexuality is a sin or that you cannot say it is wrong to have an abortion are being legislated or at least debated by civil government in certain nations, and the United States is moving in that direction. It is also interesting that the same authorities seem very open to enforcing an "antichristian" policy. The spirit of Jezebel is behind all this. The spirit of Jezebel works through governmental authority to silence the release of God's prophetic voice because it is the prophetic voice that releases the power and purposes and plans in the Earth. It is so important that we pray. The struggle is in the Heavenly realm.

Jezebel and Pastors

I believe that the spirit of Jezebel paints a target on the backs of those who are pastors. There are two things that can happen in a church when the spirit of Jezebel starts to operate. There can be such tight control that there can be no prophetic release, except the voice of Jezebel, or there can be absolutely no order, so that even the false prophet of Jezebel can prophesy in the house.

When we are talking about freedom in the church, it does not mean that anything goes. If you think like that, then you would have to say that the Apostle Paul operated under the spirit of Jezebel because he wrote a good part of the book of 1st Corinthians to a church to bring order in the middle of chaos in the area of prophecy and tongues and spiritual gifts. He taught them about true liberty. You must understand the spirit of Jezebel works in both ways. One way to stifle the true prophetic is to mingle and mix a bunch of false prophecies in it and dilute it until the people become so insecure and on such shaky ground that they do not know what is God and what is not God. The spirit of Jezebel works in that way to cause confusion and doubt.

The other way the spirit of Jezebel works is to shut down all prophetic utterance. There will be no spiritual gifts operating. It is just like putting spiritual duct tape on the prophetic voice and silencing what God wants to release in the here and now. It is the spirit of Jezebel that works through governmental authority in the church to shut down what God is doing. It is the spirit of Jezebel that works to bring disunity among leadership in churches. Jezebel works behind the scenes releasing her voice, or his voice, in destructive ways in order to remove or restrain the true voice. If the true voice is not stopped, there will be a strategic effort to undermine the credibility of the true voice so that it will not be received. Accusation, slander, gossip, and innuendoes laced with doubt and suspicion will be broadcast creating an atmosphere of doubt concerning the legitimacy of the man or woman of God carrying the message that the people really need to hear. Don't be suspicious of everyone, but you can always recognize when Jezebel is trying to stir something up. That person will always be questioning authority, looking for people who agree with them against the authority God has in place. The Jezebel spirit stirs up a person to desire an unordained and unrighteous authority in the church. This person may be in leadership but Jezebel will stir them to desire the authority of the next level. Undermining, over reacting, and magnifying minor issues will be tools Jezebel places in their hands to use against the emergence of the forerunner carrying the message that will prepare the people for what God wants to do next. As you probably have, I have heard many stories of God moving powerfully in a church only to see it stifled through an elder, a deacon, a trustee, a board member, a staff member, a teacher, or a charter member who is "concerned" about what's happening in the church. The person leading the rebellion usually thinks he or she have good intentions and are doing God's will. He or she thinks they are the only one who sees the truth. They are the only one with the courage to stop things before they get out of hand. If they are not in a position to mount a stand, they will work through someone who does have such a position.

Jezebels in the Church

One pastor friend of mine is in a church in which every time the church congregation gets excited and gets going pretty good, an individual in the church stands up and starts shutting everything down. He starts a little campaign to turn the congregation against the pastor. This church has had some good men of God in that house. As I write, that church is in the middle of a struggle because the man of God that is there now is saying, "I am not leaving! Jezebel's going, this time." The problem is not with an individual himself because the spirit manifests through a person. You are not helping that person if you allow them to operate under the influence of the Jezebel. There is a long list of pastors with broken hearts who have fallen prey to

> *Nevertheless I have a few things against you, because you allow that woman Jezebel, who calls herself a prophetess, to teach and seduce My servants to commit sexual immorality and eat things sacrificed to idols. And I gave her time to repent of her sexual immorality, and she did not repent. Indeed I will cast her into a sickbed, and those who commit adultery with her into great tribulation, unless they repent of their deeds. I will kill her children with death, and all the churches shall know that I am He who searches the minds and hearts. And I will give to each one of you according to your works.*
> *Revelation 2: 20-23*

the spirit of Jezebel. They have the forerunner anointing, and the spirit of Elijah wants to develop that new wine skin in them to bring about what God wants to do, but they have become handcuffed and silenced by the spirit of Jezebel that still operates today. The spirit of Jezebel creates an environment where the pastor and/or prophetic voice is not trusted or is pressured not to release the word necessary to bring about the needed change. Another course of action for this spirit is to influence the true prophetic voice to work outside of God's authority to release a word creating disunity in another way.

The Seducer

The spirit of Jezebel operates and attacks the prophetic voice in different ways, and one way is through seduction. In Revelation Two,

Jesus is talking to the church at Thyatira. It is interesting here that we see the heart of the Lord. He even gave Jezebel space to repent! He does not want any to perish, but there comes a time when he says, "Spirit of Jezebel, no more."

Notice that in the church at Thyatira there was a person with the spirit of Jezebel teaching who was a self-proclaimed prophetess. I can use my computer to make business cards that say I am an apostle, or a prophet, and you can, too. Having a card in your billfold does not make you an apostle, prophet or an evangelist. It does not make you a pastor or a teacher. Being one of these means the call of God is on your life and that you are anointed of God to do what the call demands of you. You do not have to put your name up in lights or on a business card for others to know it. If the authority of God is operating in someone's life, people will recognize it. I am just encouraging you not to get caught up in self promotion. The Devil is not frightened by your card but by your call.

The teaching of the self-proclaimed prophetess in Thyatira resulted in the people under her teaching being seduced into sin. You can tell what kind of fruit the teacher produces by what is reproduced in the people's lives who are feeding on what is being taught. When Jezebel talked, people started practicing idolatry and committing sexual immorality. Realize that the spirit of Jezebel will try to work against governmental authority in the church, in the nation, in the city, and in the home, in the area of sexual immorality and idolatry. It is a sensual, seductive spirit that tries to get the governmental authority to align with Jezebel's plans so that they then compromise, become manipulated, trapped, and begin decreeing what Jezebel wants.

Idolatry

Be aware that there are churches with well-meaning people who are tearing the church apart thinking they are doing the will of God. In reality, they are under the deception of the spirit of Jezebel. Idolatry always accompanies this spirit. What is idolatry? When you put anyone or anything between you and God that controls and dictates your devotional life, then you are idolizing that person or thing.

Jezebel attacks the character of governmental authority through accusation and seduction. There can be physical attacks against individuals. There can be financial attacks, even on entire nations. Governmentally, the spirit of Jezebel can suffocate and stifle, and cause a nation to move out from under the favor of God. What is the result? The result is economic woes.

One hundred and fifty years or so ago, the country of Haiti made a covenant to commit their island nation to Satan. It is the most impoverished nation in the Western Hemisphere. I know; I have been there; I have seen it. It is terrible, but it is the result of being under a demonic stronghold.

Remember, God uses the forerunner with the prophetic voice to lift up and support the kingly governmental anointing to release and carry out the plans and purposes of God in the Earth. Jezebel, in order to stop the work of the prophetic, will try to get the governmental authorities in a situation of

> Do not swallow every hook that floats by. Do not march in every parade that comes down the street. Do not clap at every song that somebody sings.

compromise, so they can be handcuffed to do her bidding instead of the bidding of the Lord. That is what happened to Ahab and Herod; it is what Jezebel wants to do today.

Don't Be Paranoid

I do not want you to be paranoid. I do not want you to be suspicious. Just simply be discerning. Look at the fruit of the people who are over you and teach you, and be discerning. You do not have to receive every word that is spoken over you. You just need to be wise and discerning.

> I have gotten a word sometimes that I thought was going to be for the church body or somebody else, but because I stopped and asked, I found out that it was for *me!*

Jesus said to be wise as serpents and as harmless as doves. It is so important to remember His very words, because when God starts pouring out and intensifying the forerunner anointing and the prophetic element in the church, there will be an increase in the enemy's attacks to try to mix and mingle the false in with the true or try to shut the anointing down altogether. Quite honestly, you need to pray for those who carry leadership authority that they will walk in wisdom, so there can be a secure protective environment, yet one with liberty and freedom for the Lord to release what He wants to release, when He wants to release it.

Sometimes it may be that you have a word that may be for some other individual. Learn to pray, "Lord, who is this for?" God prepares the preparer first. So, anytime you receive a prophetic word, corporately or individually, first of all, it needs to be run through your own life to make sure the preparer is prepared. If you are not prepared, do not release it to somebody else. Maintain order and balance, because you want the Holy Spirit to captain your ship, keep it in the middle of God's river, and steer it in the direction God wants it to move. We have a responsibility not to let Jezebel on board.

God can raise up a prophetic voice corporately. If a congregation can get in prophetic agreement and really get in the flow of what God is speaking and understand how God wants to use them, do you understand the incredible authority and power that they could carry, even in this nation? On the day of Pentecost, the disciples were are all in one accord in one place, and the Holy Spirit came in power. They began to utter what the Holy Spirit wanted them to utter, and the result was a major paradigm shift in the Kingdom. It shook the world. That is what the forerunner anointing empowers a person or a congregation to do, to shake the world.

Be Healed and Advance

There may have been times in days gone by when you have been in different settings or churches and saw the two extremes. You might have been where everything goes and everything went because of it! There was the mixing and mingling of the false and the true, and you may have been confused and disillusioned because of it. The Lord wants to set you free from disillusionment. He wants to bring clarity to your confusion. You may have been in a very strict, legalistic, controlling environment, where the spirit of Jezebel had a chokehold and you were afraid even to breathe. You might have been afraid to lift a hand. You might have been afraid to share a word of encouragement with someone. Now, I am not talking about godly fear, I am talking about spirit of Jezebel induced fear, and you may have the claw marks of Jezebel on you. That fear drove you away from the Lord, and that fear is not of God and is not the result of the Holy Spirit.

Now is the time to let the Lord heal you, and realize it is not a person's face that you should associate with the spirit of Jezebel. It is the spirit *behind* that person. We wrestle not against flesh and blood. You need to release the bitterness associated with those events or that person and begin to bless them. Ask God to move and work in their lives. Realize there is a balance. There is a place of order and protection and security. So, just let the Holy Spirit massage your spirit, and rub the Balm of Gilead, that healing oil into you. Choose to advance and move into your God given destiny. You can do it!

A Personal Prayer

Father God, I thank you for your word. I thank you, Heavenly Father, that you are my King, so I am safe and secure under your covering. You are a king who will never be compromised by the spirit of Jezebel; so, Lord, help me stay close to your heart. Lord, help me to walk in the levels of authority that I have been given in integrity, in wisdom, and in courage. Lord, I also pray for our nation that the chokehold and suffocation of the spirit of Jezebel might be removed. Lord, I pray that you would move and work across our nation apostolically and spiritually among your people to bring together that voice that you can use that is pure enough, that is powerful enough, to overthrow the spirit of Jezebel that has suffocated and stifled what you want to do in our country. Lord, help me to know the portion that I carry. Lord, I pray that you will bring about an overthrow in the Heavenlies so that there can be the release of your blessing in the earthly. So, God, teach me. Show me your ways Lord. I thank you, Lord, and I bless your name. In Jesus name, amen.

Chapter Seventeen

The Message of the Kingdom

The Kingdom is not just about Charismatics, Pentecostals, Baptists, Presbyterians, Episcopalians, Methodists, or members of the Church of Christ. The Kingdom of God transcends us all and is greater than us all. The forerunner anointing always carries a kingdom message.

John the Baptist came saying, "Repent, the Kingdom of Heaven is at hand!" Jesus later taught that the time of the law and the prophet was until John, and then He began preaching the Kingdom of God is at hand. That term "is at hand" is important. Hold your hand out. When something is at hand, it means that you can touch it. It is within reach. It is right here. It is right now. It is nearby. It is close. It is within your grasp. When John the Baptist came as the forerunner to Jesus prior to His first coming, he came saying, "Heaven's kingdom is within reach now. It's here. It's within reach." We find that in Matthew 3.

John, the forerunner, came carrying the message of the Kingdom of Heaven. He was put in prison. In Mark 1:14, after John was put in prison, Jesus came to Galilee preaching the Gospel of the Kingdom of God. What was Jesus now preaching? "The Kingdom of Heaven is at hand. The times are fulfilled. The Kingdom of God is here."

> Now after John was put in prison, Jesus came to Galilee, preaching the gospel of the kingdom of God, and saying, "The time is fulfilled, and the kingdom of God is at hand. Repent, and believe in the gospel."
> Mark 1:14

It is interesting what Jesus said about the time being fulfilled. God had worked in human history, and now a line of demarcation had been drawn, and things were about to shift and change. Until that time, things were about the law and the prophets, but now the Kingdom of God was within reach. When Jesus went to the Cross and with His dying breath said, "It is finished," He commended His spirit back to the Father. Heaven touched the Earth and the Kingdom of God became an on-going reality, because what was necessary to be done was accomplished at the Cross. When He said, "It is finished!", he was talking about the summation of things necessary in order for there to be the restoration of *all* things.

The Kingdom and Restoration

> But He said to them, "I must preach the kingdom of God to the other cities also, because for this purpose I have been sent."
> Luke 4:43

At the core of restoration of all things is an understanding of the Kingdom of God. What we read in Luke 4:43 is very powerful. Jesus said, "I must preach the Gospel of the Kingdom of God to all the other cities because for this purpose I have been sent." What cities was he referring to? He was referring to the cities throughout Israel. He was sent first to the scattered sheep of the house of Israel. He sent his disciples out into the cities of Israel. Occasionally, He ministered outside that context when the situations presented themselves in the Father's plan for him, but primarily he came ministering to the household of Israel.

> **Must**
> It is necessary, to have to, often implying inevitability, often as in the plan of God.

He said, "I must preach." The word "must" carries the idea of moral necessity. Jesus is saying, "It is incumbent upon me. I must do this, preach the Kingdom of God to other cities because for this purpose, I have been sent." You need to have an understanding of what was on the heart of Jesus about preaching to the cities of Israel because understanding the Kingdom and the concept of the restoration of all things is important in order to see the big picture. If we do not get the big picture, we will try to make our little piece of the puzzle the whole puzzle.

The concept of the restoration of all things goes all the way back to the Garden of Eden. In Genesis 1, you read how God created Adam out of the dust of the ground. God formed Adam out of a lump of dirt, and when He breathed into Adam, Adam became awake, aware, and alive! The first face that Adam ever saw was the face of God. The first

151

voice that Adam ever heard was the voice of God. The first conscious awareness that Adam ever experienced was of the presence of God. God put Adam there in the Garden to live by a river in a place called Eden which means "pleasure". There God and man communed together. Then God created Eve and presented her to Adam as his helpmate. The two of them had perfect union with each other. They had perfect union with God, a tri-unity of spirit, soul, and body in union with God the Father, God the Son, and God the Holy Spirit, man and woman in a tri-unity of unity together. That is the way God created it in the beginning.

> Then God said, "Let Us make man in Our image, according to Our likeness; let them have dominion over the fish of the sea, over the birds of the air, and over the cattle, over all the earth and over every creeping thing that creeps on the earth." So God created man in His own image; in the image of God He created him; male and female He created them. Then God blessed them, and God said to them, "Be fruitful and multiply; fill the earth and subdue it; have dominion over the fish of the sea, over the birds of the air, and over every living thing that moves on the earth." Genesis 1:26-28

God told them to be fruitful and multiply to fill the Earth, but you know what He told them before that? He said, "Exercise dominion in the Earth, over the fowl of the air, the fish of the sea, the creeping things, the beasts of the field." God created man and gave Him dominion in the Earth. You cannot read Genesis without seeing that very clearly.

Kingdom and Dominion

So, God created man and put His own image in Him. Remember how God loves to fill that which is empty! The sea was empty and He filled it with fish. The sky was empty and He filled it with birds. The galaxies were empty; He filled them with planets, sun, moons and stars. The ground was empty. He filled it with grass, herb, and trees, and all kinds of fruit. Then, He formed man out of the dust of the ground and man was empty so He filled man with Himself. He made man in His own image. He wanted a son.

Luke 3 lists Christ's genealogy. In the last verse, Adam is called the Son of God. God wanted sons and daughters in the Earth to carry

His glory, to reflect His glory, and to exercise dominion. The Bible says in Psalm 8 that we have been made a little lower than Elohim (God). In the creative order, we are the only ones who carry God's image.

God put man and woman, who bear His image, on the Earth to be regents of the Earth. In other words, we are to exercise God's authority and carry out God's governing orders in this world, and so we do! He wanted sons and daughters everywhere, all around the globe. That is in the Book of Beginnings.

When you get to the Book of Endings, what do you see? After the redemption, after the restoration of all things, and after stepping into eternity, you see sons and daughters of God. They see His face and the curses are no more. They are living by His river. They are experiencing His presence, just like God meant them to in the beginning. They are from every nation under Heaven.

So, when Jesus said, "I must preach to the other cities," he had a covenant to fulfill. After the fall, sin entered in, and Satan became a usurper. The Bible refers to him in the New Testament as the god of this age. He is the governor over the system of this world. Now the Earth belongs to the Lord. The Psalmist says the Earth is the Lord's and the fullness thereof. But, there is a usurper that is governing the system of this world.

Adam, when he sinned, lost the authority and the right to dominion. Rule, reign, and dominion, are all Kingdom terms. So, Adam lost the power to rule and reign when Satan became the usurper. God, who knew from the foundation of the world about all this, established and began the process of the restoration of all things.

In other words, we are to get back to a place where we have the Holy Spirit in us, and we are exercising authority in Earth. When did this become possible again? It happened after the cross and on the day of Pentecost. The gift of the Father, the same gift He put inside of Adam, was poured out again, because the work was finished on the cross, and the Holy Spirit came once again to indwell God's sons and daughters.

We studied that in the forerunner message early on that John the Baptist, before Christ ever began his public ministry, started teaching people to get ready for the ministry of the Holy Spirit. We are to have the image of God and the Spirit and the breath of God inside of us so we can exercise authority in this realm of Earth. There is to be a switching of kingdoms. Every time a person is saved, they switch kingdoms!

Now, why would Jesus say in Luke 11:20 that casting out a demon was a sign of the Kingdom of God? Jesus said that because those demons were the servants of the usurper operating the

> *But if I cast out demons with the finger of God, surely the kingdom of God has come upon you. Luke 11:20*

system of this world – Satan. People are inhabited with demons that do the bidding of Satan and move in an ungodly direction. So, Jesus shows up! God in human flesh! The last Adam! And, what the first Adam lost, the last Adam came to restore and put back in its proper place.

Jesus came as God in human flesh exercising the dominion of God on the Earth. That is the reason John the Baptist could say, "Get ready, He is coming. Heaven's kingdom is right at hand." That is the reason Jesus basically was saying, "I am here, now; God's kingdom is here now." So, when He casts out a demon it is kingdom work, and the usurper has to give back ground.

Every time a person is saved, they are switching kingdoms. Paul says we are translated from the kingdom of darkness into the kingdom of the love of God's dear Son. There is a conflict in this invisible world around us between the kingdom of Satan and the Kingdom of God. Satan had his ground of authority

> *Then I heard a loud voice saying in Heaven, "Now salvation, and strength, and the kingdom of our God, and the power of His Christ have come, for the accuser of our brethren, who accused them before our God day and night, has been cast down. Revelation 12:10*

because of Adam's sin and forfeiture, and so he is always accusing people. But, when you understand the finished work of Christ, recognize that he is the King of Kings, that you have been restored to walk in the power and authority and the wisdom of God, then you too, can operate with power against the powers of darkness, cast out demons, and establish God's kingdom in the human heart.

154

The Kingdom within You

Jesus said, "The kingdom of God is within you." He said, "My kingdom is not of this world; if it were, I would fight." It is not that He did not fight – it is that He does not fight the way the world does. Oh, yes, the violent take it by force and the Kingdom of God is here and the people are pressing into it, but there is still a battle. I am telling you, when you preach the Gospel, you are wielding the sword of the spirit, and it is war, because somebody's about to switch kingdoms! So, the restoration of all things has to do with this.

> Now the Lord had said to Abram: "Get out of your country, From your family And from your father's house, To a land that I will show you. I will make you a great nation; I will bless you And make your name great; And you shall be a blessing. I will bless those who bless you, And I will curse him who curses you; And in you all the families of the earth shall be blessed."
> Genesis 12:1-3

Jesus taught about the Kingdom of God. John tells us that when you are saved and the Holy Spirit indwells you that, "Greater is He who is in you now than he who is in the world."

We are in this world, governed by the god of this age, Satan, but we are not of this world. And the One inside of us through the Spirit is greater than the one operating in the world. So the Kingdom of God is being established in the world heart by heart. God is raising up a people. God is raising up a bride. There is war, but we do not fight the way the world fights. The weapons of our warfare are not carnal, but mighty through God to the pulling down of strongholds.

> But you shall receive power when the Holy Spirit has come upon you; and you shall be witnesses to Me in Jerusalem, and in all Judea and Samaria, and to the end of the earth.
> Acts 1:8

We wrestle not against flesh and blood. The battle is not against brothers and sisters, man and woman. He said that we wrestle against principalities and powers of the host of wickedness in the heavenly places. That is where the warfare is. The Kingdom of God *now* is the invisible kingdom. It is in the heart, but it will become visible and manifest in the Earth. But, it will be a *new* Earth.

Understand that the kingdom message carried by the forerunner is not just about us. It is not just about you. It is not just about your congregation. It is about all the blood-bought, born-again believers that make up the Kingdom of God, and that is what Jesus preached. By relating the words of Jesus to us in Acts 1, Luke makes it clear to us that we will be empowered by the Holy Spirit to witness to the outermost parts of the Earth. God had made a covenant after Adam fell in the Garden. You can study it in Genesis 12. God called a man named Abram.

Abraham's Promise

As in the Father, so it is in the son. Jesus said, you have seen me, you have seen the Father. As in Abraham, so it will be seen in the seed of Abraham. What did God say to Abraham? "I want you to leave your family and your land. Then I am going to do something inside of you that will result in all, not some, but in all the families of the Earth being blessed (personal paraphrase)." It is a prophetic picture.

Abraham lived this out in his own natural life, and, by promise we know that Jesus came through his lineage. As a result, all the families of the Earth have been blessed. But, where did Jesus start in his own family? He started with the seed of Abraham. That is where he started – with Israel. There was an occasion when he said to the Syro-Phoenician woman, I cannot minister to you. I came to minister to Israel. The woman still reached his heart and got her request by pressing in and declaring that even the dogs were allowed the crumbs that fall from the Master's table. Yet Jesus knew that his focus initially was in reference to the covenant that God made to Abraham. The

> I will also give You as a light to the Gentiles, That You should be My salvation to the ends of the earth.' "
> Genesis 12:6

promise was that through Christ, the "seed" that all the families of the earth would be blessed through Abraham who became a father through faith. In other words, God never intended His work just to be about Israel. He told Abram to leave his family so that he would become a blessing to all the families of the Earth. God always had *all* the families

156

in mind. That was in the heart of God concerning restoration all along, and there are scriptures to bear that out.

It was not ever just about Israel, or just about the Jews. They were the vehicles that God used to bring the message to all the families of the Earth. It is so sad that when Jesus came into his own people they received him not. But those that did receive him, were given authority to become the sons, like Adam, the sons of God; this is restoration. They were given *exousia*, the Divine right of sonship by Father God's own authority.

Because of their status as sons and daughters they were invested with authority as Adam was. Why? So that they could be using that authority in the

Exousia (Greek) the power of authority (influence) and of right (privilege).

Earth as Adam was supposed to in order to establish God's kingdom on the Earth so that the glory of the Lord would extend from sea to shining sea. That is the reason we have the promise that in the middle of the gross darkness, the glory of the Lord shall cover the Earth. God is going to manifest His glory through his sons and daughters in whom He has invested His authority because they have received Jesus.

I believe there is restoration concerning Israel as well. Was not God's order that through the promise made to Abraham that he would establish His covenant with Abraham, raise up the Christ, and those that receive Him would become part of the Kingdom of God? We are told in Mark 11:10 that "Blessed is the kingdom of our Father, David that

Therefore, when they had come together, they asked Him, saying, "Lord, will You at this time restore the kingdom to Israel?" And He said to them, "It is not for you to know times or seasons which the Father has put in His own authority. Luke 1: 6-7

comes in the name of our Lord. Hosanna in the highest." We know when the forerunner came, the religious leaders expressed disbelief that the Messiah was on the way because they believed he would be one of their own. What did John tell them? In Matthew 3, John said,

"Therefore bear fruits worthy of repentance, and do not think to say to yourselves, 'We have Abraham as *our* father.' For I say to you that God

157

is able to raise up children to Abraham from these stones." Is it not interesting what Jesus said in Luke 13? While talking to the religious leaders, he warned them that they would not join Abraham, Isaac, and Jacob in the Kingdom of God, because they would be cast out. They refused to see the big picture.

The Time is in the Father's Hands

Jesus does not rebuke the disciples when they asked the time of restoration of the kingdom to Israel, but he does give them some correction about their focus. He simply told them that they were not to know the time. In other words, there is going to be a shifting and change in the times and the seasons when God is going to do things relative to restoration. In other words, you cannot know that; God has not revealed it. Only the Father knows that.

> There is a lot of talk about pre-millennial, post-millennial, a-millennial, pan-millennial (it will pan out), pre-trib, pos-trib, mid-trib, and pre-wrath opinions of the last days. I am telling you something, boil it down; "He is coming. Be ready. When He gets here, He is taking over."

> ... all that Jesus began both to do and teach, until the day in which He was taken up, after He through the Holy Spirit had given commandments to the apostles whom He had chosen, to whom He also presented Himself alive after His suffering by many infallible proofs, being seen by them during forty days and speaking of the things pertaining to the kingdom of God.
> Luke 1:1-3

To paraphrase what Jesus said, "All of that, the times and seasons, is in the Father's hands, but let me tell you what God is going to do for you. He is going to give you power." Is it not interesting how he answered their question about the time for Israel to be restored? He says "It is in the Father's hands, but you shall receive power after the Holy Spirit has come upon you and you shall be witnesses unto me, not only in Jerusalem. It is not going to be only an Israeli kingdom, but in Judea, Samaria, unto the uttermost parts of the Earth." Loosely speaking, that's how Jesus responded to their question.

During that forty-day period, what did Jesus preach? He taught them pertaining to the Kingdom of God. When he came on the scene at

158

the beginning of his ministry, he was preaching the Kingdom of God. Right before he ascended, he was preaching the Kingdom of God.

Do you know what He also said in the Gospel of Matthew? He said, "And this message and this Gospel shall be preached as a witness to all nations and then the end shall come." God has always had all the nations in His heart. When He saved you, put His spirit in you so that you could become a witness to others so the Kingdom of God could grow and expand, so that His dominion and authority on the Earth could grow and expand.

When God declares something is going to happen, *it is going to happen*. He made a promise to Abraham, that through Abraham, all the families of this Earth are going to be blessed. He made a promise to David, that He would raise up an heir out of David's loins that will sit on the throne of David forever.

The Beginning in the End
The End in the Beginning

It is about the Kingdom of God, the total restoration of all things. The spirit of Elijah must first come and restore all things. Peter, as a forerunner, understood that after Jesus ascended God was going to be working to bring about the restoration of all things. He preached

> Repent therefore and be converted, that your sins may be blotted out, so that times of refreshing may come from the presence of the Lord, and that He may send Jesus Christ, who was preached to you before, whom Heaven must receive until the times of restoration of all things.
> Acts 3:19-21

the Kingdom message in Chapter 3 of Acts. Peter is talking about restoration because he instructs us to repent so that we may be refreshed and restored and made ready for Jesus to come again.

In the early chapters of Genesis are written the original designs, intentions, patterns, principles, and paradigms that were in effect when God created humankind. When you get to the Book of Endings (Revelation), you find the restoration of those things. You see that God does have sons and daughters that are surrounding Him, living in His presence, living by His river, eating from His tree of life, enjoying and worshipping Him, and glorifying Him forever and ever.

It will be in a new Heaven and a new Earth, because the Bible says the former Heaven and the former Earth have passed away. But, before this Earth passes away, there will be a time when every knee will bow and every tongue will confess that Jesus Christ is Lord. Paul says, "We have all fallen short of that glory." Jesus came as the second man and the last Adam to restore us into that place where we can be divinely credentialed by the Sprit of God to be bearers of the glory of God in the Earth again. The Bible says that now the Holy Spirit working in us is transforming us from one level of glory to another level of glory, being changed from glory to glory.

I believe the Bible teaches that when Jesus comes back for his bride, she is going to be without spot, wrinkle, blemish, or any such thing. God will not fail, and He is going to purify, perfect, and raise up his bride. Adam had a bride; Eve was born out of his side. They were a perfect union, and they enjoyed perfect union with God. The last Adam also has a bride, birthed out of his side. Before it is all over he and his bride are going to enjoy perfect union with God to the glory of God the Father. The Father will have

> [19] If in this life only we have hope in Christ, we are of all men the most pitiable. [20] But now Christ is risen from the dead, and has become the first fruits of those who have fallen asleep. [21] For since by man came death, by Man also came the resurrection of the dead. [22] For as in Adam all die, even so in Christ all shall be made alive. [23] But each one in his own order: Christ the first fruits, afterward those who are Christ's at His coming. [24] Then comes the end, when He delivers the kingdom to God the Father, when He puts an end to all rule and all authority and power.
> 1 Corinthians 15: 19-24

His glorious children enjoying Him in His glorious presence. It will all be glory by and by.

More Revelation Needed

I do not know all the ends and outs of it. I am not worried about it. But I do know that God is restoring all things. I want to grow in my revelation. I want to grow in my understanding of it. God is establishing His kingdom, and it is not a worldly kingdom, but it is a kingdom that will overthrow the system of this world. I want you to understand that Jesus came preaching the kingdom of God. He left preaching the kingdom of God, and when he comes back, it will be to culminate the Kingdom of God and hand it over to his Father for the Father's glory.

In First Corinthians 15, Paul is teaching on the Resurrection. Verse 19 tells us that there is more than what you see down here. You see, we live by faith, not by sight. We operate in an invisible realm, but one day faith will become sight. In verse 21, Paul is talking about Adam and the second man. Who is that second man? That second man is Jesus.

Verses 22 and 23 tells us that he is coming back! Verse 24 has to do with sequential thought; then something is going to happen. Christ is going to come, and then comes the end. Well, at least one thing we can see is that the second coming is not the end in itself. The second coming precedes the end. The end is specified occurring when he delivers the kingdom to God the Father, and when he puts an end to all rule, authority, and power.

Jesus is coming back! Then, he is going to deliver, hand over, and present to the Father, the kingdom. When that happens, an end will come to all rule, all authority, and all power because all things will be summed up in Christ and given to the Father. But then, we see another time word; for he must reign *until*. There is your time word, *until*, for he must reign *until* he has put all enemies under his feet.

God is working right now to restore all things. He is beautifying his bride. He is adding to the kingdom. He is adding to His family, His sons and daughters in the Earth.

Be Ready to be Surprised

The first year I was called to preach, I thought I understood the whole book of Revelation, and I thought, "Well, everything else will be easy from now." I read books written by people who *seemed* to perfectly understood it. I was ready! But, we see through a glass – how? We see

> *For now we see in a mirror, dimly, but then face to face.*
> *1 Corinthians 13:12*

through it dimly, so we cannot get overly dogmatic and think that everybody else is wrong, and we are right. Remember, when Jesus came, the people who were supposed to be teaching people to get ready for Him did not even recognize Him. I will be surprised if all of us are not very surprised at how all this works out.

Remember also the situation in the Garden of Eden, when Adam walked face to face with God. That is what is going to happen when Jesus comes back. Paul also tells us in 2 Corinthians that he knew of a man, (more than likely himself), called up into the third Heaven. He stated that this had happened fifteen years earlier which would place the experience prior to his writing of 1 Corinthians. In other words, here is a man who is called up into the third Heaven and he has a glimpse of eternity. Yet, he still writes, "…we see in a mirror dimly."

Do not think you see it just like it is! Remember what Paul wrote in 1 Corinthians 2:9. We cannot imagine how awesomely wonderful, how incredibly beautiful it is going to be. He is restoring all things. He is bringing His family together, and then there will come a day when Jesus comes back. John, the forerunner, preached about the second coming before Jesus came at the first coming when he said, "He will gather his wheat into his barn, and all the chaff he will burn with unquenchable fire." There is going to be a gathering together when He comes. Jesus gathered together all His people during His first coming.

We find out in the Book of the Revelation that in the new Heaven and new Earth we will all be enjoying with Him what Adam and Eve did in the beginning. The people will be there from every kindred, every tribe, and from every nation under Heaven. So, the kingdom is bigger than we are. Jesus said, "It's like seed, and it starts growing and it grows and expands."

Sometimes we ask, 'Lord, will you restore the kingdom of Israel now?' But it is bigger than Israel. It is bigger than you. Yes, God used the nation of Israel to birth it, and He is going to keep the covenant, but the whole purpose behind it is that all the nations would know the Kingdom of God.

He is coming! Are you ready? Are you a kingdom person? Are you carrying any judgment toward other parts of the kingdom? Are you a family person? Do you understand the concept of the family of God, the household of faith, being adopted as sons and daughters? Do you have anything in your heart toward brothers or sisters?

Who is your king? If I were to ask your best friend who is the king of your life indicated by the way you live, what would your best friend say? Are you living for the King of Kings and the Lord of Lords?

A Personal Prayer

Father God, I just pray right now that the kingdom message will find a resting place in my heart. Lord, I will be the first one to confess I do not understand how all the dots line up about all the end-time events, but I do know, Lord, you are coming back, and I do know you are going to gather us together, and I do know that Satan going to be ultimately overthrown. I do know that I am going to get to be with you forever, and I do know all that is good.

So, Lord, I want to live with these simple truths embedded in my heart and mind so that the words of my mouth and the meditations of my heart will be pleasing to you. Help me to be a kingdom person, Lord. Help me to have your heart for the nations. Help me to realize you have engraved your image inside me. You have given me your Spirit, and He is the promise of the Father, so that I can fulfill the last commandment to go to the nations. From my neighbor to all the nations, that is your heart, Lord, help that be my heart. Kingdom of God come! Will of God be done! I thank you Lord Jesus, and I bless your name, amen!

Chapter Eighteen

Following then Forerunning

Every forerunner ends up where he does because others before him ended up where they did. Every new invention is based on the success of older ones. We always are building on something that existed before we did. We are here because a father and a mother existed before we did. Most of the knowledge we gain is from others who gained it first. New knowledge is knowledge gained added to knowledge already attained. What is new revelation to you probably has been given to someone else somewhere else and possibly centuries earlier. But what you carry is uniquely yours.

> New knowledge is knowledge gained added to knowledge already attained.

The components that have merged together that have made your personal history belong to you and no one else has that same history. God will reveal things to you about you that differ from what He has ever told anyone else because there has never been another you! Every conversation He has ever had with you is uniquely yours. God orchestrates our lives together creating a richness for each of us because we are here with the rest of us. Sound confusing? Simply put, we are supposed to be connected. Our histories and our destinies converge together to make each of us better because the rest of us are here. This is family!

The forerunner must always remember that where his run for God takes him is always rooted in where God had him. Your future is linked to your past. Where you are going to is inescapably linked to where you are coming from. The in-between parts are called school. The place where lessons learned can be turned into successes achieved. Before we strike out on our own, we must first appreciate and honor those whom God has used to bring us to the place of release. Before we unfold our wings and soar, we must first thank God for all those nest builders, brooders, feeders, protectors, and scouts who have flown their own missions and have lived to tell of their journey to the regions beyond.

Learning to Lead by Following

We are not prepared to lead until we are first willing to follow. This is part of the preparation process for the preparers we are calling forerunners. Submission and honor to authority prepares our hearts for promotion. Jesus spent the first thirty years of his life in a rather obscure place working under Joseph's leadership. Elisha who followed Elijah and received the double portion did so after he had faithfully served and submitted to the generational leader before him. Forerunners lead people into new places but they do so with the same principles that all the forerunners before them used. The Lord will not allow our advance into the new places at the expense of our character. When a forerunner has a major character lapse it can actually be used of the enemy to close gates that have been opened and to clutter paths that have been cleared.

> We are not prepared to lead until we are first willing to follow.

Learning to follow effectively builds a depth of character that will enable the future forerunner to be an effective leader. This part of God's preparatory process also develops within us the need to be team players. It also keeps us from falling prey to the lone ranger mentality that is always detrimental to the cause of Christ. This is the Day of the Saints when people in the pews are being equipped and connecting with others in the body and being mutually edified. This insures a movement toward the fullness of Christ with the Bride that will enable her to arise in purity and power ready for her Bridegroom to return.

By spending time serving in supporting roles, the future forerunner will develop an appreciation for all those who will want to support, encourage, and play a part in fulfilling God-given vision. I had served as a pastor for five years in a small church before we relocated to Memphis to attend seminary. I was soon to discover that we do not know nearly as much about what we need as the Lord does. Memphis would prove to be a time of learning to learn.

Mentored in Memphis

Mikki and I moved to Memphis to attend seminary. I thought that we would get settled in, and I would find a church to pastor. After all, I was "experienced". I wouldn't call it that now, but that's what I called it then. As it turned out, I became an intern in a large church in Memphis. The church had a program where seminary students who were hired would serve as helpers to the church staff. I ended up doing this for most of the years I was in seminary and I am so grateful that the Lord chose this as part of the plan for my life. It was a great benefit to me to serve under staff who were also serving under senior staff who were serving under the Senior Pastor. I learned so many principles, lessons, and took tests that I would not have been exposed to in another context. I learned that we are not really fit to lead until we have proven that we have learned to follow. It is in following that one is truly learning to lead. A forerunner has to be led by the Holy Spirit.

> Submission in the natural helps us learn submission in the spiritual.

Submission in the natural helps us learn submission in the spiritual. It is in this way that parents are to raise their children in the nurture and admonition of the Lord. They model following the Lord, and the child follows them.

Needed: Granddaddy Pastors

As I write this book I am serving as Senior Pastor at a church of about 1500 in attendance surrounded by an incredibly loving and supportive staff and church family. Before the baton was placed in my hand to serve as Senior Pastor, I had the privilege of serving Pastor Henry Melton as his associate. Though I had been serving as a Senior Pastor for years, the Lord spoke to my heart to go and serve Pastor Henry trusting that the Lord would let him know when the time was right to pass the baton. I said yes to the Lord and to Bro. Henry's request to come serve him in preparation for

> There is a difference in taking a baton and receiving a baton. A proper exchange is about timing, preparation, and cooperation.

succeeding him. Eleven months later he asked me to receive the baton from him and assume the role of Senior Pastor. There is a difference in taking a baton and receiving a baton. A proper exchange is about timing, preparation, and cooperation. It is all about timing so that the baton will not be dropped because of late timing or jerked away prematurely before transition can occur. This has been a beautiful and fruitful transition for both of us. The congregation and I view Pastor Henry as our Granddaddy Pastor. There is such a need in the body for Granddaddy pastors. He is my greatest encourager in the church and has allowed me to lead while always being available to help in any way that I might ask.

I did have some people who tried to persuade me not to go as Associate Pastor and demand that I become the Senior Pastor immediately. Even after I became Associate Pastor a few people tried to encourage me to put pressure on my Pastor to step aside and make room for the new man on the scene. I expressed my firm disagreement with these suggestions and shared that it was not to be mentioned to me again. I knew this was a wrong spirit operating, and I refused to be a party to the Absalom spirit. I knew that the way I treated my Pastor would sow seeds for how I would be treated as Pastor. I also knew my Pastor's heart and knew it was pure. How arrogant it would have been for me to show up and demand the place of a godly man who had served for 42 faithful years as the church's undershepherd. I realized that Faith Tabernacle Church had been blessed for many years before Eddie Lawrence ever showed up. What a great step of faith that Pastor Henry was taking to place the baton in my hand. By saying "yes" to God's call to serve Pastor Henry, I was saying that I trusted him to be my pastor. By placing the baton in my hand, he was saying that he now trusted me to be his pastor. What has made this work is the father-son relationship that exists between us. A father always rejoices when his son is able to go farther than he has gone. A father has only pure motives when he gives direction to his son because he loves him and wants what is best for him. A son will not be suspicious of his father and vice versa. They are in a family relationship. Our congregation now

167

enjoys the ministry of a father who feeds them and leads them and the ministry of a grandfather who encourages and covers them with love. We all are so excited about this because we feel it is God's way. The Bible is so clear. Humble yourself under the mighty hand of God, and He will exalt you in due time. We are also reminded that God resists the proud but gives grace to the humble.

Mutual Honor

Forerunning does not mean we are to bowl over those who have paved the way before us. This is dishonorable, and the Lord cannot bless it. When Jesus came to John to be baptized they both responded with honor to each other. John honorably argued that Jesus should baptize him, but Jesus said that it was the right thing for John to baptize him. He submitted himself to the ministry of John, even though he and John both knew that his work would go beyond the point where John would be able to go. There are no hints of jealousy, competition, or jockeying for position to be seen between them. This is our model to follow when we are called upon to lead others through transition. We must press into what awaits us in the Spirit while honoring those the Lord has used before our arrival. When this is done, and we are able to step into our Jordan, then the heavens will opened, and the Father's approval will be witnessed.

> He submitted himself to the ministry of John, even though he and John both knew that his work would go beyond the point where John would be able to go.

Our guard must always be up against the zeal of youth or the pride of life that could wrongly cause us to trample upon the godly work of the pioneers whom we follow. I am not saying that change should not occur; it should! I am not saying that we always agree with everything done by those who go before. I am saying that the Lord will honor us when we give honor to others to whom it is due. The Sauls must put up their spears when the Davids show up and the Absaloms must wait patiently refusing to ascend to the place of the Davids before their time. Trying manipulation to make a place for yourself will actually cause you to be limited in how far you can go and how much you can accomplish. The Lord is not only concerned about His work being done but is also concerned about how it is done. Our motives must be pure so that our work can be pure.

> Trying manipulation to make a place for yourself will actually cause you to be limited in how far you can go and how much you can accomplish.

By learning to follow we learn to lead. By learning to serve we learn to appreciate the role that every believer plays in the body. We gain a greater ability to submit and follow the Holy Spirit when we submit and follow those the Holy Spirit has placed over our lives as leaders.

Ready, Set, ???

This is the place where spiritual fathers and mothers have the opportunity to help shape a generation of forerunners who will take the baton and run farther and faster than we have. Those who are spiritual fathers and mothers must petition Heavenly Father for the wisdom to know when our children are ready to advance. Premature promotion can be tragic. Holding people back who are equipped and ready and are getting Heaven's nod to proceed can produce frustration and temptation to disregard the role of honor. Being sensitive to the "due time" of the Lord helps honor to be preserved in the house of the Lord and to keep faithful forerunners clearing the paths for the next generation. We all need godly people who can help us know we the Lord is pulling the trigger for us to Go!

Just as a pregnant Mom gets restless and ready to deliver before the baby is mature enough to be delivered, we also tend to get restless and ready to advance before the Lord opens the door before us. This can be very frustrating but understand that it is during this time that character is being formed and wisdom is being attained. Both of these, character and wisdom, are necessary for a forerunner as he or she starts clearing the thickets and moving through the briars to uncharted territory. It is very important for the forerunner sitting in the

> Premature promotion can be tragic.

waiting room to do more than passively wait. This is the time to aggressively seek the heart of God so that their own heart can begin to

169

reflect His heart. The frustration and restlessness will often cause unresolved and unsettled character issues to surface and be dealt with through the power of the Holy Spirit and the blood of Jesus. Its not just stepping on home plate and scoring a run that is important. Running the bases correctly is just as important if the run scored is to counted. Knowing that people are coming behind you should put a little shock into your system to be serious about where you are going and how you are doing.

> Knowing that people are coming behind you should put a little cover shock into your system to be serious about where you are going and how you are doing.

Parents and Pioneers

Every parent is a forerunner in the sense that they are preparing the way for their children. We should evaluate where the highway we are building for our kids to travel on is leading them. I want to forerun my natural and spiritual children into the land of the destiny of God where the river of God flows and the Spirit of God is moving in loving power.

It may be that there is a need for repentance in your life in regard to dishonor toward someone who pioneered before you? Could there be any disdain that you are carrying toward those foot soldiers of yesterday's generation? If so, you will not progress down the path of the true pioneers until you get into alignment with God's protocol for pioneering. There are no shortcuts when it comes to humility and honor, submission and obedience. Jesus himself said that he only did what he saw the Father doing. He demonstrated for us the paradigm for progression in the area of forerunning. After all, he was the ultimate forerunner who became the author (pioneer) and the finisher of our faith. He went the distance, and he will insure that you too will go the distance if you will just keep your eyes on him.

> Then Jerusalem, all Judea, and all the region around the Jordan went out to him. Matthew 3:5

The Gathering of the Followers

The Father enjoys gathering the hungry together and setting a table before them where they are served bread from Heaven. He wants

170

people to hear what they need to hear. When a message is released to His messengers, and they are released to share it, then the Lord will give them a platform. It may be on a hillside out on the edge of the wilderness but the people will come. The Father will see to that. The Spirit will draw them within earshot of his messenger. The forerunner anointing is also an anointing causing people to gather, to bring people together. God anointed John, think about it, this crazy guy who comes out of the woods and starts preaching out in the wilderness, and all of a sudden, folks start traveling where he is to hear what he has to say! John was carrying an anointing that caused people, when they heard what he had to say, to know they were hearing from God. The word spread and people started coming from everywhere to be under the mantle of John, to hear this message from God through John. Because they heard and confessed their sins their lives were changed. They were baptized as a baptism of repentance. They were baptized as a sign that they were changing the way they lived.

Chapter 1 of Genesis tells us that God gathered all the waters together and called them seas. The heart and nature of God from the very beginning of creation has been to gather together. In Acts, Chapter 2, we read that God brought the disciples together, and they were filled with the Holy Spirit. Then what happened? They were scattered to preach the word. He scatters those gathered so that they can bring others together. So people gathered from all around Jerusalem and Judea to see and hear John and Jesus. Scripture tells us that is the heart of God to gather people together

When the Day of Pentecost had fully come, they were all with one accord in one place.

Acts 2:1

Therefore they that were scattered abroad went everywhere preaching the word. Acts 8:4

And when this sound occurred, the multitude came together...

Acts 8: 6

And there were dwelling at Jerusalem Jews, devout men, out of every nation under Heaven. Now when this was noised abroad, the multitude came together, and were confounded ...

Acts 2: 5-7

God is gathering together. Why? He is gathering together to release the forerunner anointing so that the people who are gathered

171

together are changed and then go out and gather more people together so that *they* can be changed. Going out or sending out is an apostolic ministry. To be apostolic means to be send out. The reason there is a sending out is so that there can be the bringing in. That is part of the operation of the forerunner anointing.

In Acts 2, Scripture tells us that people gathered from everywhere. When God starts doing something different, people start coming. The hungry come. Why? They come because what they have been hungering and thirsting for is to be under the anointing and to be prepared to live for Christ. They want to step into their destiny.

The curious come. Who are the curious? The curious are those people thinking, "Well, I am not sure, but I am going to check it out." Then they come and sit a while. Then they may leave and say, "You know, I do not know. I just do not think that is for me." But they come, do some rubber necking, take a few steps, and the next thing you know, they are in the river of God![Q] They become the hungry.

> Then the scribes and Pharisees who were from Jerusalem came to Jesus, saying, "Why do your disciples transgress the tradition of the elders? For they do not wash their hands when they eat bread."
> Matthew 15:1

The hungry come, the curious come, and also the critical come. Some people just get tired of hearing about a move of God, and they want to come see it so they can know how to criticize it and how to judge it. Critical, judgmental religion shows up, just as it did when the Pharisees questioned the activities of John and the disciples of Jesus. Criticism is directed at all whom God chooses to use. The forerunner must endure criticism. Smite the shepherd and the sheep will scatter is still a satanic strategy. Question the messenger's reputation and the message will be questioned. When this occurs, we must avoid reacting in flesh and trust the Lord to guard our lives and ministries. We search our hearts to make sure there is no ground for the enemy to base his accusations. A

[Q] *Is there someone whom you know that is beginning to express curiosity toward the things of the Lord? What could you do to encourage them?*

daily lifestyle of repentance will keep your reputation from being ruined. The enemy knows that by seducing someone to ruin a reputation that he stalls the forerunner's progress into destiny. I don't want to live in the land of what could have been, do you?

The Joints Coming Together

We must not allow criticism to keep us from gathering together and going with God. Jesus is the head of the church and our orders are to come from headquarters. If we cast the vision that is birthed in our own heart, that is just an idea. But the vision that comes from God, it imparts life, because without that kind of vision, what happens to the people? The people perish, literally, they start losing moral restraints. In other words, they start getting into sin. So, sin is the primary barrier to unity.

In Psalms 22, we have a prophetic picture of the crucifixion. Last year, as I was meditating and studying on Psalm 22, I saw something I had not seen before. I believe that everything that Jesus went through on the cross, he went through literally in his physical body. Currently, he is seated at the Father's right hand in his glorified body. We are now his body in the earth. We are the body of Christ. So I believe that everything he went through on the cross, which his physical body was subjected to, has a message for his body in the Earth now, the church. The one thing that caught my attention had to do with his joints being pulled out of joint. They were dislocated. I started praying and asking the Lord what it means spiritually that his bones were pulled out of joint. None of his bones were broken, but his bones were disjointed. What is that a picture of?

> I am poured out like water, And all My bones are out of joint; My heart is like wax; It has melted within Me.
> Ps 22:14

As I prayed on this I felt the Lord whisper to me, "Go to Ephesians, Chapter 4. I went there and it read about the five-fold ministry: the apostle, the prophet, the evangelist, the pastor, and the teacher and how they have been given to the church to equip the saints to do the work of the ministry. As I read on it says, "So the body of Christ can come into maturity – the love of Christ receiving that which every joint supplies." I sensed revelation at that moment. The Lord helped me to see that when Jesus died on the cross, his literal body, his physical body whose joints were dislocated and separated did so as he hung there under the weight of our sin. What did he bear on the cross? He bore our sin.

> from whom the whole body, joined and knit together by what every joint supplies, according to the effective working by which every part does its share, causes growth of the body for the edifying of itself in love. Eph 4:16

Our sin was placed on his body on the tree. When we think of his body now, here on the Earth, his church, what does sin do to the body? Sin causes the joints to be separated.

> Let's stay away from the sin that keeps us apart.

We as members of the body of Christ, have something to give to the body. We have something that we can supply. The love of Christ is to flow from one joint to the other. He gives the office gifts of the church, the five-fold ministry to mature the body, to grow up the body, so that the bones can start connecting, the joints can start getting together in that unity and oneness so that the church can start getting the full supply of what God is wanting to provide to her through the various joints and places of connection. Sin is what causes the joints of the body of Christ here in the Earth to become dislocated and separated so that you are not receiving from me what you could receive, and I am not receiving from you what I could receive. Sin causes us to be separated. But when there is unity, those joints are connecting. We are connecting in the spirit, and there is a divine flow of the love of Christ enabling the body to grow in power.

If you pull all the bones out of joint in a person's body, they cannot walk or move at all. They are just a loose collection of bone and muscle unable to get anything done. They are a mere mass of tissue that cannot be supported because the bones won't get together and stay together. But when those bones get together and connect at the joint, then that body can rise up, can stand up and that is the picture in Ephesians 4 of coming into the fullness of the stature of Christ, of the body of Christ rising up and walking in the anointing, power, and love of God to fully express the body and bride of Christ in the earth. It's interesting when you get to Ephesians 5, Paul tells us that when Jesus comes back, the body, the bride is going to be without spot, blemish, wrinkle, or any such thing. So that tells me that before Jesus comes back, there is going to be the move of the Spirit of God to bring unity in the body. There has been enough of being label conscious.

Don't you want to be a faithful follower of Christ all the days of your life? Don't you want to be counted trustworthy so that you can be a forerunner who motivates others to follow the ultimate forerunner himself, the Lord Jesus Christ? Heaven awaits us only because Jesus waded through the swamp of sin, scaled the unscalable mountain of death, and planted the flag of resurrection victory on its peak. What is there to stop us if we simply keep looking unto Jesus the author and finisher of our faith? Just follow him, and you will end up in the middle of the destiny that God placed in you when you were in your mother's womb. Run, forerunner, run! Don't look back! Run! Run! Run!

A Personal Prayer

Dear Father, help me to run the course you have set before me. I want to be forerunner who is following Jesus. I desire that my life be expended for your honor and your glory. Give me the grace, resolve, and passion I need to keep on keeping on. May I be an encouragement to other forerunners. May I be found a faithful carrier of the portion with which you have entrusted me. Lord, help me to desire and promote unity in your body. Help me to be willing to connect with others so that the Bride can stand and be strong. Help me to help them. Help me to want to help them. Help me to lay all aside to make you the heart of all that I do. You are the reason that I exist. I praise you and bless you for saving me, calling me, and enlisting me as a forerunner. Help me to run, Lord, help me to run. In Jesus name, amen.

Chapter Nineteen

The Sons of Jacob

On June 6, 1944, the United States and the allies launched a massive campaign to take back France and the rest of occupied Europe. They stormed the beaches of Normandy with the determination to liberate France. Thousands of soldiers who came off the boats that were being rammed ashore gave their lives. The first ones off were facing the greatest danger as the enemy fired machine guns, dropped mortars, and threw grenades into their midst. Man after man fell, and blood soaked the sands of the foreign shore that became the open coffin of thousands of lifeless bodies. At last, enough men made it through this real time nightmare to take over the beaches, strongholds, and out posts of the enemy. From there they stormed throughout the rest of France and finally throughout all of the European countries that were under the Nazi boot.

These storming soldiers, who were the first ones to step in the line of enemy fire, were true forerunners. Many of them laid down their lives in order that those behind them might advance further than they did. Still others were injured, maimed, and marked for life by enemy fire and some friendly fire. They were all determined to move forward. There were people who needed liberated from a hostile power. They went with the order of their commander and chief in their hearts. When it was all over they could say "Mission Accomplished." The people of France were shouting jubilantly the good news of freedom, and the commander and chief was saying "Well done!"

Forerunning Those Who
Are Not Yet Following

In addition to those who rejoiced at what had happened, these forerunners had also benefited the people who did not believe in the war effort, people who refused to help in the war effort, and people who even aided the enemy. As a matter of fact, the surviving enemy soldiers themselves were blessed due to this liberation wrought by brave forerunners invading the land they had seized. Part of the portion a forerunner carries is for those who do not choose to follow them. Some may never appreciate the forerunner, others will eventually recognize the value of what they accomplished, and then some will have their lives turned around for the good because they embrace what the forerunner has done.

Joseph the Forerunner

The Old Testament contains the story of a forerunner who also experienced doing what he did for people who rejected him. He was even forced into it against his will. Joseph, the son of Jacob, represents this facet of forerunning for those who do not want to follow. Space does not allow for a full exposition of all the truths and principles that are available for the forerunner in the life of Joseph, but I hope that you will be encouraged by the following principles.

The Suffering Principle

> In entering into the sufferings of Christ you are prepared for greater levels of anointing and authority.

As a Forerunner, you will experience a measure of suffering. If you suffer with him, you will reign with him. In entering into the sufferings of Christ you are prepared for greater levels of anointing and authority to abide upon your life; if not in this life, then certainly in the life to come. The Martyr's crown will shine brightly because the martyr has suffered greatly. We we step into the sufferings of Christ, we position ourselves for remptive purposes to be fulfilled. The Lord has ordained that redemption comes by means of suffering. Particularly, suffering the just for the unjust. Joseph's life was one marked by suffering. The pit, Potiphar's house, a prison, and finally the palace was a sequence of one kind of suffering to the next. The WWII soldiers I mentioned are examples of those who suffer so others want have to. They show us how courage can overcome fear. Pioneers always carry the bruises, cuts, and blows that are landed by a path that needs to be cleared or an enemy that needs to be uprooted. Joseph was bruised by his brothers, but from God's perspective, he was bruised for his brothers. So was Jesus the greatest forerunner ever.

As you step into your destiny, there will be some suffering along the way. If someone promises you differently, don't hold that promise too tightly. Paul assured young Timothy that living a godly life would bring persecution. It was true for Jesus; therefore, should the servant boast a more blessed path than his master. Don't become disillusioned when tough times come. Remember, that the Lord is greater than our tough times. The life of Joseph proves to us that God is not uninvolved in our tough times. On the finished side of Joseph's suffering, he even told his brothers that what they had meant for evil, God had meant for good. He actually uses the things that we think are holding us back to move us forward. By the way, only God can do this. Our Father does not cause Evil but He works in spite of it.

The Revelation Principle

Joseph received a revelation that his brothers did not receive. His revelation came to him in a form of a dream. His dream showed him being exalted above his family. This was unnatural because he was the younger at the time. In his dream, he saw his brothers sheaves bowing before his sheaves. He also dreamed another dream where he saw the sun, moon, and eleven stars bowing before him. His brothers and his father rebuked him for implying that he would reign over them. However, Joseph's dreams contain a preview of his future. These snapshots of destiny would prove to be anchors for his soul in the coming months and years.

> But when his brothers saw that their father loved him more than all his brothers, they hated him and could not speak peaceably to him.
> Genesis 37:4

The dream of the sheaves certainly carried a picture of things to come in Joseph's future. It would be wheat gathered and stored that would bring his brothers to bow before him would provide food in famine for his family and his nation. As a young man, he did not understand the significance of all of this, yet, it was a revelation of his destiny. It pictured a harvest that he would oversee that provided deliverance for the multitudes. It is easy to see that Joseph was a prophetic type of Christ in many ways. When Jesus returns there will be a gathering of his wheat into his barns and every knee will bow before him.

> And his brothers said to him, "Shall you indeed reign over us? Or shall you indeed have dominion over us?" So they hated him even more for his dreams and for his words.
> Genesis 37:8

178

The dream of the sun, moon, and stars pictured government and authority. They represent those luminaries that towered overhead and pictured Joseph's rise to power and his family prostrating before him. He did not understand it fully as a young man, but it was part of his destiny. His brothers and fathers were able to understand what the dreams would indicate. He may have faired better had he not gone public so soon, especially in the way that he did. Nevertheless, he had been given revelation from God that broadcasted his future destiny. His brothers became jealous and viewed their brother as a mere dreamer with his head in the clouds. From God's perspective, Joseph was chosen as a forerunner to go before his brothers and lead them to where he was. This started a twenty-year journey to the place called destiny. Seems like a long time, but many live their whole life and do not make it to this place. Hang on to the revelation that God gives you. It contains the word that will encourage you during the days, months, and years of preparation that will test you. It will often contain details of what your destiny will look like.

The Opposite Principle

Gunpowder and fire when mixed together create an explosion. In the right context when they are controlled correctly, they can be used to move mountains and clear paths. However, when used unwisely, they become very

> Revelation from God is a powerful thing and contains the ability to bring about destiny.

dangerous to those who handle it. Revelation from God is a powerful thing and contains the ability to bring about destiny. However, it must be handled wisely. Not everyone needs to know about the revelation God has given you about your destiny. Some might discourage you instead of encouraging you. Joseph had been given a revelation of his destiny. He did not share it wisely with his older brothers. His excitement mixed with their jealously created quite an explosive set of circumstances. They could not even speak peaceably to him.

Joseph learned first hand about the opposite principle. He saw through a dream that his brothers would bow before him while he was exalted above them. However, the next thing Joseph experienced was being thrown in a pit. At the top of the pit, he could hear the verbal plans of his brothers who were conspiring to kill him. There they stood towering over him with murder in their hearts. It was the opposite of what he was told would happen. Many times we experience the opposite principle operating in our lives after we have received revelation from the Lord. This extreme test of our faith certainly teaches us that revelation from the Lord brings opposition from the pits of Hell.

This often happens when a believer begins receiving revelation of God given destiny concerning the power and authority they have truly been given as a son of God. When he shares it with his brothers, who have been around longer than he has, they often began to mock, react, reject, and eventually alienate their dreaming brother. In addition, if one is not careful to guard his heart, he will end up in a pit and his brothers will end up with blood on their hands. As I write this paragraph, I am only 20 minutes removed from a telephone call concerning a pastor who was being pressured to resign the Church he pastored simply because he had taken steps into the spirit-filled life and believed that God would heal sick people when they were anointed with oil and prayed for in faith. His excitement of flowing in the new revelation of God's power and authority was being met with opposition. He was happy about God's desire to heal; yet, he was being confronted by those willing to see Christ's body torn apart rather than walk in a new realm of revelation.

Often the greatest enemies to God given revelation come from within the fallen human heart. Pride deceives us into believing that we could not possibly be wrong. When this happens, there is a reunion among the cousins in the works

> Often the greatest enemies to God given revelation come from within the fallen human heart.

of flesh family. Jealousy, envy, hatred, malice, vindictiveness, deception, rejection, slander, and character assassination team up to do their dirty work against the forerunner trying to lead others into a deeper place with God. These forces cause the "Sons of Jacob" to draw the conclusion to remove Joseph out of their sight. Their jealous controlling hearts whispered, "I don't like this revelation he is sharing so let's get him out of our sight so that we do not have to see him, hear him, or be in relationship with him." Remember, these were brothers to Joseph. They were all sons of Jacob, yet they were willing to sacrifice their brother to strangers, rather than considering some revelation that seemed strange to them. It is sad when the familiar and comfortable wins out over that which challenges and stretches us and which could launch us into our destiny. Choosing the familiar has at times opened the door to familiar spirits. This can start a demonic lineage that a family has to struggle against for generations. Being rejected by one's brothers and sisters is painful. Some of you reading these words know the pain caused by those who prefer fight over light.

Fortunately, Joseph stayed humble and bitter free through all of this. We can humble ourselves or we can be humbled. There is usually a going down before there is a going up. The way up is down. Joseph started in the pit but his humility would take him to the palace before the story would conclude.

The Merchandise Principle

The unseen hand of God was working through all that Joseph went through, though it could hardly be noticed at the time. God's hand moved upon Joseph's brothers preventing their plans of murder. They chose to sell him away out of their sight. They devised a story that left their father with the conclusion that Joseph had been devoured by a wild beast. While Jacob wept over his son's death, unknown to him, Joseph was being led in fetters to the land of Egypt where he would be sold into slavery. He was sold to the Ishmaelites. These distant cousins saw Joseph as an opportunity that would personally profit them. They carried in their DNA, as did the sons of Jacob the tendency to shortcut the purposes of God by making decisions in the flesh. This is how Abraham had birthed their grandfather Ishmael.

> *Therefore humble yourselves under the mighty hand of God, that He may exalt you in due time, 1 Peter 5:6*

> *And being found in appearance as a man, He humbled Himself and became obedient to the point of death, even the death of the cross. Philippians 2:8*

When you are carrying revelation and you are rejected by those who should be supporting you, be careful of those who may come along and try to merchandise you. They want you only for what they can get out of you. I'm not just talking about money. Often a rejected people will pull in a rejected leader so that he can be their trophy and they can feed their hurts by watching him hurt. This is motivated by bitterness that has risen out of unhealed emotional wounds. After all, the Ishmaelites came from a Ishmael who had also been cast out of Abraham's family. They carried rejection in their DNA and they were more than willing to take in another member of Abraham's clan who was being cast out, especially since they could make a few shekels off him. They knew from the moment they bought Joseph that he would only be a temporary resident with them. They were not interested in relationship with him. They were only interested in how they could use him to entertain them. Perhaps they saw him as an opportunity to land a few strikes to settle an old score, and make a few bucks in the process. We must always be careful that the rejection we experience does not cause us to loose discernment about whom and what we should embrace.

The Seduction Principle

Joseph was forced to start his life over as a slave in a strange place. He had gone from favored son to a slave. What he still had was a revelation of his destiny. God knew he would be elevated to the highest place, so to prepare him, he allowed him to experience the lowest place. Though the favor of his earthly father was removed from him, the favor of his Heavenly Father continued to be with him. He experienced favor in the middle of slavery. Potiphar, the Egyptian master who had bought Joseph, prospered because of the presence of Joseph in his house.

> Joseph chose purity though it cost him prison.

One day while Potiphar was away, his wife made a move on Joseph. Her lust for this young slave in her house culminated in an invitation for Joseph to lie with her. Instead, he ran from her. In her scorn for Joseph's resistance, she charged him with attempted rape, and he was falsely imprisoned. He was taken down again in the natural but God was going to use it to prepare him for what he would later carry. Thus far, he had learned to speak the Egyptian language, do Egyptian accounting, and oversee Egyptian slaves. In prison, he learned how to manage the whole prison system. All of this would be used later in his life to save a nation. God was using the Devil's strategy against Joseph to train him to reign. Had Joseph said "yes" to the seductive invitation of Potiphar's wife, he would have most likely forfeited his opportunity to say "yes" to his destiny. Sometimes a single "yes" at the wrong time can sidetrack your destiny. Sexual temptation is a powerful tool of the enemy to arouse our natural desires and deceive us into derailing our destiny. The lesser "yes" can topple the greater "yes." Joseph chose purity though it cost him prison. Being confined in the will of God will prove much more beneficial than indulging the flesh by crossing sexual boundaries. How many broken homes exist today in christian families due to a man or a woman saying "yes" to the voice of seduction? It is sad when awaiting destiny is exchanged for momentary pleasure. Esau is not the only one to sell his birthright for a "bowl of porridge." When the voice of seduction whispers in your ears, run, run, run!

The Burden Principle

Becoming a slave introduces a person to a life of bearing burdens for other people. Joseph was sold into a life of forced labor, but he made the best of it. He did not choose to be a slave, but he did choose to be a slave that would honor his God. He also made a choice that one burden he would not bear would be the burden of bitterness. He chose to focus on what could be, where he was, instead of what was, where he had been. The Psalmist tells us during this time of Joseph's life the word of the Lord tested him. Joseph held to the word and the word held to him. Bitterness and unforgiveness could have cast him into another pit, the one called depression, but it did not because Joseph kept his eyes on God, and not his problems. Also, there was another burden Joseph was carrying. Joseph bore on his shoulders the burden of a slave but he always carried in his heart a burden for his brothers. His destiny involved his brothers. As he held to his destiny, he held to his brothers.

Often our warfare reveals our destiny. When we run into the Devil, it can be evidence that we are headed in the right direction. If we never run into him, it may be because we are running with him. Do not disregard the possibility, that the people who have rejected your pressing ahead in the Lord, may be part of your destiny. We

> Often our warfare reveals our destiny.

must remain open for the Lord to burden our hearts for those who oppose us. This is the heart of Jesus. At the cross, we find him expressing love for those who are cursing him. A good sign that our heart is freed from unforgiveness and bitterness is that we carry a burden for our opposers. This enables it to become redemptive because love never fails. Do not let bitterness remove your brothers from your heart. They have the same father; they really are your brothers. When they become hungry enough, they will come to you because you will have more than you need.

The Divine Surprise Principle

When the day came for Joseph's brothers to bow before him as the Prime Minister of Egypt, he had been well groomed by the Holy Spirit to see God's purposes in all he had gone through. Joseph was surprised by God and the sons of Jacob were surprised by Joseph. God holds veto power over Satan's plan for your life. The brothers that you are tempted to hate, because they have hated you, and the brothers that you are tempted to reject, because they have rejected you, need someone to help them. This someone must be willing to wade through pain and rejection to prepare for them what they are going to need when famine strikes their hearts. This is part of the call of a forerunner—to bear the unbearable and to love the unlovable.

God is still the God of the divine surprise. More than once, He has used a pharaoh to raise up His next deliverer. He is so confident in His power as God that He allowed baby Moses to be nestled and cradled in the arms of the daughter of the Pharaoh who had enslaved His people. He is so confident that He allowed the hope of the whole nation of Nineveh to be swallowed into the belly of a great fish. He is so confident and powerful that He allowed the little boy who would be Israel's favored King to play the harp at the feet of the man who would try to kill him, a spear throwing demonized king, Saul. He is so filled with surprises that He entrusted the preaching of the Gospel to the whole Gentile world to a man who had been fighting tooth and toenail against the church. He is still full of surprises.

God still transforms persecutors into preachers.

How many of you reading this book once fought against what you now fight for? How many of you once taught vehemently against the move of the Spirit that you are now a part of? Rememver when God did something that moved you out of the place of famine into the place of favor. We should not be so surprised, if day by day, we see faces of brothers standing with us, that only yesterday stood against us. The Apostles, were a little slow in welcoming Saul of Tarsus, until they discovered that God had gloriously saved him. He was the one who had tried to track each of them to their death. Saul, the Pharisee of Pharisees, was changed in Paul

184

the Apostle to the Gentiles. God still transforms persecutors into preachers. God still transforms, young would be forerunners, with hearts filled with dreams, into kings with great authority and power.

One of the greatest surprises occurs when Joseph's brothers, who did not recognize his destiny of exaltation at the first, could not see Joseph for it at the last. When he got his revelation, he was just a kid that had a big dream of authority and dominion. In the beginning, they could not see dominion and authority, they could only see Joseph. In the end, they could not see Joseph, they could only see dominion and authority. What a grand turn around. He foreran right into the place called destiny and his whole family ended up following him. His suffering resulted in their salvation. Sound familiar?

Even God's only begotten Son experienced being humbled, rejected, misunderstood, misquoted, and outright attacked. He too went into a pit; he too carried the marks caused by the sins of those he was destined to save. He even preached to the spirits in prison after he died, whatever that phrase means. He came unto his own and they did not receive him. However, when he comes back, he will be seen in the dominion, authority, and might of the Lord of Lord's and the King of Kings. God has a way of turning things around before it's all done. He did it for the sons of Jacob. He will do the same for you. Keep on forerunning and hold the dreams of destiny that God has given you in your heart. Remember that suffering leads to reigning and humility leads to exaltation.

And He will reign over the house of Jacob forever, and of His kingdom there will be no end." Luke 1:33

A Personal Prayer

Dear Father, I praise you for working all things together for good in my life. Thank you so much for orchestrating and weaving the circumstances of my life together so that your purposes will be fulfilled. I submit to the plan you have mapped out for my life. I am willing to forerun for the sake of others, even those who are unwilling at this time to follow. I pray that you would bless those who curse me and give me the grace to do good to those who mistreat me. Through your grace and power, I pray that you would break all the power of rejection

185

off my life. Help me to properly respond to suffering, and to realize that I will rule and reign to a greater degree if I keep my heart free from bitterness and unforgiveness. Help me to always walk in humility and submission to you, Lord Jesus, because you are the King of Kings, you are the Lord of Lords, and you will rule and reign forever! By faith I choose to step into my God ordained destiny. In Jesus name, amen!

Bibliography of Sources

A Dictionary of Biblical Languages
Greek New Testament by James Swanson
© 1997, Logos Research Systems, Inc.
All rights reserved. Second edition, 2001

Biblesoft's New Exhaustive Strong's Numbers and Concordance with Expanded Greek-Hebrew Dictionary. Copyright © 1994, 2003 Biblesoft, Inc. and International Bible Translators, Inc.

Enhanced Strong's Lexicon
© 1995 Woodside Bible Fellowship

Harper's Bible Dictionary
P.J. Achtemeier, Harper & Row, & Society of Biblical Literature (1985). (1st ed.) San Francisco, Harper & Row

Merriam-Webster's Collegiate Dictionary, 10th Edition

The American Heritage ® Dictionary of the English Language, Fourth Edition.

The Complete Word Study Dictionary: New Testament © 1992 by AMG International, Inc. Revised Edition, 1993

The IVP Bible Background Commentary: New Testament
Craig S. Keener, InterVarsity Press
Downers Grove, Illinois 60515
© 1993 by Craig S. Keener

The Moody Handbook of Theology
Moody Press, Chicago
© 1989 by Paul P. Enns

The New King James Version. Copyright © 1982 by Thomas Nelson, Inc. Used by permission. All rights reserved.

CONTACT AND RESOURCE INFORMATION

ORDERING RESOURCES ONLINE:

If you are interested in further resources including workbooks, teaching series, preaching materials, and audio messages, please contact us at firstbreathministries.com

QUESTIONS & COMMENTS:

We would enjoy hearing from you concerning how this study has impacted your life or concerning questions you may have. You may contact us online at the firstbreathministries.com through the contact button or by postal mail at:

First Breath Ministries
P.O. Box 1228
Killen, Alabama 35645

AUDIO MESSAGES ONLINE:

To listen to one of Dr. Lawrence's recent messages, visit online at firstbreathministries.com. Simply click on the recent sermon button on the bottom left hand corner of the home page.

CONFERENCES AND SPEAKING ENGAGEMENTS

To look into the possibility of scheduling Eddie Lawrence for a speaking engagement, please contact him through the website at Firstbreathministries.com or at the postal address listed above.